QUICK
REFERENCE

WORLD ATLAS

Contents

Quick Reference World Atlas
Copyright © 1995 by Rand McNally & Company.

Printed in the United States of America

Library of Congress Catalog Number: 95-067031

World Political Information Table

This table gives the area, population, population density, political status, capital, and predominant languages for every country in the world. The political units listed are categorized by political status in the form of government column of the table, as follows: A—independent countries; B—internally independent political entities which are under the protection of another country in matters of defense and foreign affairs; C—colonies and other dependent political units; and D—the major administrative subdivisions of Australia, Canada, China, the United Kingdom, and the United States. For comparison, the table also includes the continents and the world. All footnotes appear at the end of the table.

The populations are estimates for January 1, 1994, made by Rand McNally on the basis of official data, United Nations estimates, and other available information. Area figures include inland water.

Region or Political Division	Area Sq. Mi.	Est. Pop. 1/1/94	Pop. Per. Sq. Mi.	Form of Government and Ruling Power	Capital	Predominant Languages
Afars and Issas see Djibouti						
† Afghanistan	251,826	16,595,000	66	Islamic republic ... A	Kābul	Dari, Pashto, Uzbek, Turkmen
Africa	11,700,000	683,700,000	58			
Alabama	52,423	4,202,000	80	State (U.S.) ... D	Montgomery	English
Alaska	656,424	597,000	0.9	State (U.S.) ... D	Juneau	English, indigenous
† Albania	11,100	3,424,000	308	Republic ... A	Tiranë	Albanian, Greek
Alberta	255,287	2,599,000	10	Province (Canada) ... D	Edmonton	English
† Algeria	919,595	26,780,000	29	Provisional military government ... A	Algiers (El Djazaïr)	Arabic, Berber dialects, French
American Samoa	77	53,000	688	Unincorporated territory (U.S.) ... C	Pago Pago	Samoan, English
† Andorra	175	58,000	331	Parliamentary co-principality (Spanish and French) ... B	Andorra	Catalan, Spanish (Castilian), French
† Angola	481,354	11,040,000	23	Republic ... A	Luanda	Portuguese, indigenous
Anguilla	35	7,000	200	Dependent territory (U.K. protection) ... B	The Valley	English
Anhui	53,668	58,850,000	1,097	Province (China) ... D	Hefei	Chinese (Mandarin)
Antarctica	5,400,000	(1)				
† Antigua and Barbuda	171	64,000	374	Parliamentary state ... A	St. John's	English, local dialects
† Argentina	1,073,519	33,635,000	31	Republic ... A	Buenos Aires and Viedma (4)	Spanish, English, Italian, German, French
Arizona	114,006	3,943,000	35	State (U.S.) ... D	Phoenix	English
Arkansas	53,182	2,438,000	46	State (U.S.) ... D	Little Rock	English
† Armenia	11,506	3,743,000	325	Republic ... A	Yerevan	Armenian, Russian
Aruba	75	68,000	907	Self-governing territory (Netherlands protection) ... B	Oranjestad	Dutch, Papiamento, English, Spanish
Ascension	34	1,000	29	Dependency (St. Helena) ... C	Georgetown	English
Asia	17,300,000	3,385,900,000	196			
† Australia	2,966,155	17,950,000	6.1	Federal parliamentary state ... A	Canberra	English, indigenous
Australian Capital Territory	927	303,000	327	Territory (Australia) ... D	Canberra	English
† Austria	32,377	7,913,000	244	Federal republic ... A	Vienna (Wien)	German
† Azerbaijan	33,436	7,481,000	224	Republic ... A	Baku (Bakı)	Azeri, Russian, Armenian
† Bahamas	5,382	270,000	50	Parliamentary state ... A	Nassau	English, Creole
† Bahrain	267	572,000	2,142	Monarchy ... A	Al Manāmah	Arabic, English, Farsi, Urdu
† Bangladesh	55,598	115,240,000	2,073	Republic ... A	Dhaka	Bangla, English
† Barbados	166	260,000	1,566	Parliamentary state ... A	Bridgetown	English
Beijing (Peking)	6,487	11,365,000	1,752	Autonomous city (China) ... D	Beijing (Peking)	Chinese (Mandarin)
† Belarus	80,155	10,380,000	129	Republic ... A	Minsk	Belarussian, Russian
Belau see Palau						
† Belgium	11,783	10,050,000	853	Constitutional monarchy ... A	Brussels (Bruxelles)	Dutch (Flemish), French, German
† Belize	8,866	205,000	23	Parliamentary state ... A	Belmopan	English, Spanish, Mayan, Garifuna
† Benin	43,475	5,292,000	122	Republic ... A	Porto-Novo and Cotonou	French, Fon, Yoruba, indigenous
Bermuda	21	76,000	3,619	Dependent territory (U.K.) ... C	Hamilton	English
† Bhutan	17,954	1,707,000	95	Monarchy (Indian protection) ... B	Thimphu	Dzongkha, Tibetan and Nepalese dialects
† Bolivia	424,165	7,582,000	18	Republic ... A	La Paz and Sucre	Aymara, Quechua, Spanish
† Bosnia and Herzegovina	19,741	4,442,000	225	Republic ... A	Sarajevo	Serbo-Croatian
† Botswana	224,711	1,424,000	6.3	Republic ... A	Gaborone	English, Tswana
† Brazil	3,286,500	151,310,000	46	Federal republic ... A	Brasília	Portuguese, Spanish, English, French
British Columbia	365,948	3,354,000	9.2	Province (Canada) ... D	Victoria	English
British Indian Ocean Territory	23	(1)		Dependent territory (U.K.) ... C		English
British Virgin Islands	59	13,000	220	Dependent territory (U.K.) ... C	Road Town	English
† Brunei	2,226	279,000	125	Monarchy ... A	Bandar Seri Begawan	Malay, English, Chinese
† Bulgaria	42,855	8,813,000	206	Republic ... A	Sofia (Sofiya)	Bulgarian, Turkish
† Burkina Faso	105,869	9,922,000	94	Republic ... A	Ouagadougou	French, indigenous
Burma see Myanmar						
† Burundi	10,745	6,015,000	560	Republic ... A	Bujumbura	French, Kirundi, Swahili
California	163,707	31,905,000	195	State (U.S.) ... D	Sacramento	English
† Cambodia	69,898	10,010,000	143	Transitional government ... A	Phnum Pénh (Phnom Penh)	Khmer, French
† Cameroon	183,568	12,845,000	70	Republic ... A	Yaoundé	English, French, indigenous
† Canada	3,849,674	27,950,000	7.3	Federal parliamentary state ... A	Ottawa	English, French
† Cape Verde	1,557	414,000	266	Republic ... A	Praia	Portuguese, Crioulo
Cayman Islands	100	32,000	320	Dependent territory (U.K.) ... C	George Town	English
† Central African Republic	240,535	3,089,000	13	Republic ... A	Bangui	French, Sango, Arabic, indigenous
Ceylon see Sri Lanka						
† Chad	495,755	6,149,000	12	Republic ... A	N'Djamena	Arabic, French, indigenous
Channel Islands	75	149,000	1,987	Dependent territory (U.K.) ... B		English, French
† Chile	292,135	13,795,000	47	Republic ... A	Santiago	Spanish
† China (excl. Taiwan)	3,689,631	1,184,060,000	321	Socialist republic ... A	Beijing (Peking)	Chinese dialects

Region or Political Division	Area Sq. Mi.	Est. Pop. 1/1/94	Pop. Per. Sq. Mi.	Form of Government and Ruling Power		Capital	Predominant Languages
Christmas Island	52	1,300	25	External territory (Australia)	C	The Settlement	English, Chinese, Malay
Cocos (Keeling) Islands	5.4	600	111	Territory (Australia)	C	West Island	English, Cocos-Malay, Malay
† Colombia	440,831	35,085,000	80	Republic	A	Bogotá	Spanish
Colorado	104,100	3,528,000	34	State (U.S.)	D	Denver	English
† Comoros (excl. Mayotte)	863	508,000	589	Federal Islamic republic	A	Moroni	Arabic, French, Comoran
† Congo	132,047	2,403,000	18	Republic	A	Brazzaville	French, Lingala, Kikongo, indigenous
Connecticut	5,544	3,272,000	590	State (U.S.)	D	Hartford	English
Cook Islands	91	19,000	209	Self-governing territory (New Zealand protection)	B	Avarua	English, Maori
† Costa Rica	19,730	3,285,000	166	Republic	A	San José	Spanish
† Cote d'Ivoire	124,518	13,930,000	112	Republic	A	Abidjan and Yamoussoukro (4)	French, Dioula and other indigenous
† Croatia	21,829	4,796,000	220	Republic	A	Zagreb	Serbo-Croatian
† Cuba	42,804	11,015,000	257	Socialist republic	A	Havana (La Habana)	Spanish
† Cyprus	2,276	574,000	252	Republic	A	Nicosia (Levkosía)	Greek, English
Cyprus, North (2)	1,295	193,000	149	Republic	A	Nicosia (Lefkoşa)	Turkish
† Czech Republic	30,450	10,400,000	342	Republic	A	Prague (Praha)	Czech, Slovak
Delaware	2,489	700,000	281	State (U.S.)	D	Dover	English
† Denmark	16,639	5,181,000	311	Constitutional monarchy	A	Copenhagen (København)	Danish
District of Columbia	68	576,000	8,471	Federal district (U.S.)	D	Washington	English
† Djibouti	8,958	579,000	65	Republic	A	Djibouti	French, Arabic, Somali, Afar
† Dominica	305	87,000	285	Republic	A	Roseau	English, French
† Dominican Republic	18,704	7,715,000	412	Republic	A	Santo Domingo	Spanish
† Ecuador	105,037	10,515,000	100	Republic	A	Quito	Spanish, Quechua, indigenous
† Egypt	386,662	56,820,000	147	Socialist republic	A	Cairo (Al Qāhirah)	Arabic
Ellice Islands see Tuvalu							
† El Salvador	8,124	5,179,000	637	Republic	A	San Salvador	Spanish, Nahua
England	50,352	48,320,000	960	Administrative division (U.K.)	D	London	English
† Equatorial Guinea	10,831	379,000	35	Republic	A	Malabo	Spanish, indigenous, English
† Eritrea	36,170	3,540,000	98	Republic	A	Asmera	Tigre, Kunama, Cushitic dialects, Nora Bana, Arabic
† Estonia	17,413	1,608,000	92	Republic	A	Tallinn	Estonian, Latvian, Lithuanian, Russian
† Ethiopia	446,953	54,170,000	121	Provisional military government	A	Addis Ababa	Amharic, Tigrinya, Orominga, Guaraginga, Somali, Arabic
Europe	3,800,000	709,300,000	187				
Faeroe Islands	540	48,000	89	Self-governing territory (Danish protection)	B	Tórshavn	Danish, Faroese
Falkland Islands (3)	4,700	2,200	0.5	Dependent territory (U.K.)	C	Stanley	English
† Fiji	7,056	759,000	108	Republic	A	Suva	English, Fijian, Hindustani
† Finland	130,559	5,056,000	39	Republic	A	Helsinki (Helsingfors)	Finnish, Swedish, Lapp, Russian
Florida	65,758	13,855,000	211	State (U.S.)	D	Tallahassee	English
† France (excl. Overseas Departments)	211,208	57,680,000	273	Republic	A	Paris	French
French Guiana	35,135	134,000	3.8	Overseas department (France)	C	Cayenne	French
French Polynesia	1,359	211,000	155	Overseas territory (France)	C	Papeete	French, Tahitian
Fujian	46,332	31,375,000	677	Province (China)	D	Fuzhou	Chinese dialects
† Gabon	103,347	1,127,000	11	Republic	A	Libreville	French, Fang, indigenous
† Gambia	4,127	919,000	223	Republic	A	Banjul	English, Malinke, Wolof, Fula, indigenous
Gansu	173,746	23,445,000	135	Province (China)	D	Lanzhou	Chinese (Mandarin), Mongolian, Tibetan dialects
Gaza Strip	146	745,000	5,103	Israeli territory with limited self-government			Arabic
Georgia	59,441	6,875,000	116	State (U.S.)	D	Atlanta	English
† Georgia	26,911	5,646,000	210	Republic	A	Tbilisi	Georgian, Russian, Armenian, Azeri
† Germany	137,822	80,930,000	587	Federal republic	A	Berlin and Bonn	German
† Ghana	92,098	16,595,000	180	Republic	A	Accra	English, Akan and other indigenous
Gibraltar	2.3	32,000	13,913	Dependent territory (U.K.)	C	Gibraltar	English, Spanish, Italian, Portuguese, Russian
Gilbert Islands see Kiribati							
Golan Heights	454	29,000	64	Occupied by Israel			Arabic, Hebrew
Great Britain see United Kingdom							
† Greece	50,949	10,500,000	206	Republic	A	Athens (Athínai)	Greek, English, French
Greenland	840,004	57,000	0.1	Self-governing territory (Danish protection)	B	Godthåb	Danish, Greenlandic, Inuit dialects
† Grenada	133	91,000	684	Parliamentary state	A	St. George's	English, French
Guadeloupe (incl. Dependencies)	687	424,000	617	Overseas department (France)	C	Basse-Terre	French, Creole
Guam	209	147,000	703	Unincorporated territory (U.S.)	C	Agana	English, Chamorro, Japanese
Guangdong	68,726	65,830,000	958	Province (China)	D	Guangzhou (Canton)	Chinese dialects, Miao-Yao
Guangxi Zhuangzu	91,236	44,285,000	485	Autonomous region (China)	D	Nanning	Chinese dialects, Thai, Miao-Yao
† Guatemala	42,042	10,510,000	250	Republic	A	Guatemala	Spanish, Amerindian
Guernsey (incl. Dependencies)	30	63,000	2,100	Crown dependency (U.K. protection)	B	St. Peter Port	English, French
† Guinea	94,926	6,274,000	66	Provisional military government	A	Conakry	French, indigenous
† Guinea-Bissau	13,948	1,078,000	77	Republic	A	Bissau	Portuguese, Crioulo, indigenous
Guizhou	65,637	33,985,000	518	Province (China)	D	Guiyang	Chinese (Mandarin), Thai, Miao-Yao
† Guyana	83,000	732,000	8.8	Republic	A	Georgetown	English, indigenous
Hainan	13,127	6,867,000	523	Province (China)	D	Haikou	Chinese, Min, Tai
† Haiti	10,714	6,411,000	598	Provisional military government	A	Port-au-Prince	Creole, French
Hawaii	10,932	1,167,000	107	State (U.S.)	D	Honolulu	English, Hawaiian, Japanese
Hebei	73,359	63,940,000	872	Province (China)	D	Shijiazhuang	Chinese (Mandarin)
Heilongjiang	181,082	36,945,000	204	Province (China)	D	Harbin	Chinese dialects, Mongolian, Tungus
Henan	64,479	89,520,000	1,388	Province (China)	D	Zhengzhou	Chinese (Mandarin)
Holland see Netherlands							
† Honduras	43,277	5,206,000	120	Republic	A	Tegucigalpa	Spanish, indigenous
Hong Kong	414	5,890,000	14,227	Chinese territory under British administration	C	Victoria (Hong Kong)	Chinese (Cantonese), English, Putonghua
Hubei	72,356	56,480,000	781	Province (China)	D	Wuhan	Chinese dialects
Hunan	81,081	63,580,000	784	Province (China)	D	Changsha	Chinese dialects, Miao-Yao
† Hungary	35,919	10,295,000	287	Republic	A	Budapest	Hungarian
† Iceland	39,769	262,000	6.6	Republic	A	Reykjavík	Icelandic
Idaho	83,574	1,089,000	13	State (U.S.)	D	Boise	English
Illinois	57,918	11,750,000	203	State (U.S.)	D	Springfield	English
† India (incl. part of Jammu and Kashmir)	1,237,062	906,770,000	733	Federal republic	A	New Delhi	English, Hindi, Telugu, Bengali, indigenous
Indiana	36,420	5,733,000	157	State (U.S.)	D	Indianapolis	English
† Indonesia	752,410	198,810,000	264	Republic	A	Jakarta	Bahasa Indonesia (Malay), English, Dutch, indigenous

Region or Political Division	Area Sq. Mi.	Est. Pop. 1/1/94	Pop. Per. Sq. Mi.	Form of Government and Ruling Power	Capital	Predominant Languages
Iowa	56,276	2,827,000	50	State (U.S.) .... D	Des Moines	English
† Iran	632,457	63,940,000	101	Islamic republic .... A	Tehrān	Farsi, Turkish dialects, Kurdish
† Iraq	169,235	19,335,000	114	Republic .... A	Baghdād	Arabic, Kurdish, Assyrian, Armenian
† Ireland	27,137	3,563,000	131	Republic .... A	Dublin (Baile Átha Cliath)	English, Irish Gaelic
Isle of Man	221	72,000	326	Crown dependency (U.K. protection) .... B	Douglas	English, Manx Gaelic
† Israel (excl. Occupied Areas)	8,019	4,950,000	617	Republic .... A	Jerusalem (Yerushalayim)	Hebrew, Arabic
† Italy	116,324	56,670,000	487	Republic .... A	Rome (Roma)	Italian, German, French, Slovene
Ivory Coast see Cote d'Ivoire	....	....		....		
† Jamaica	4,244	2,538,000	598	Parliamentary state .... A	Kingston	English, Creole
† Japan	145,870	124,840,000	856	Constitutional monarchy .... A	Tōkyō	Japanese
Jersey	45	86,000	1,911	Crown dependency (U.K. protection) .... B	St. Helier	English, French
Jiangsu	39,614	70,210,000	1,772	Province (China) .... D	Nanjing (Nanking)	Chinese dialects
Jiangxi	64,325	39,550,000	615	Province (China) .... D	Nanchang	Chinese dialects
Jilin	72,201	25,815,000	358	Province (China) .... D	Changchun	Chinese (Mandarin), Mongolian, Korean
† Jordan	35,135	3,858,000	110	Constitutional monarchy .... A	'Ammān	Arabic
Kansas	82,282	2,568,000	31	State (U.S.) .... D	Topeka	English
† Kazakhstan	1,049,156	17,190,000	16	Republic .... A	Alma-Ata (Almaty) and Akmola (4)	Kazakh, Russian
Kentucky	40,411	3,813,000	94	State (U.S.) .... D	Frankfort	English
† Kenya	224,961	28,280,000	126	Republic .... A	Nairobi	English, Swahili, indigenous
Kiribati	313	77,000	246	Republic .... A	Bairiki	English, Gilbertese
† Korea, North	46,540	22,735,000	489	Socialist republic .... A	Pyŏngyang	Korean
† Korea, South	38,230	44,250,000	1,157	Republic .... A	Seoul (Sŏul)	Korean
† Kuwait	6,880	1,734,000	252	Constitutional monarchy .... A	Kuwait	Arabic, English
† Kyrgyzstan	76,641	4,645,000	61	Republic .... A	Bishkek	Kirghiz, Russian
† Laos	91,429	4,601,000	50	Socialist republic .... A	Viangchan (Vientiane)	Lao, French, English
† Latvia	24,595	2,556,000	104	Republic .... A	Rīga	Latvian, Russian, Lithuanian
† Lebanon	4,015	3,566,000	888	Republic .... A	Beirut (Bayrūt)	Arabic, French, Armenian, English
† Lesotho	11,720	1,907,000	163	Constitutional monarchy under military rule .. A	Maseru	English, Sesotho, Zulu, Xhosa
Liaoning	56,255	41,325,000	735	Province (China) .... D	Shenyang	Chinese (Mandarin), Mongolian
† Liberia	38,250	2,901,000	76	Republic .... A	Monrovia	English, indigenous
† Libya	679,362	4,917,000	7.2	Socialist republic .... A	Tripoli (Ṭarābulus)	Arabic
† Liechtenstein	62	30,000	484	Constitutional monarchy .... A	Vaduz	German
† Lithuania	25,212	3,777,000	150	Republic .... A	Vilnius	Lithuanian, Polish, Russian
Louisiana	51,843	4,332,000	84	State (U.S.) .... D	Baton Rouge	English
† Luxembourg	998	401,000	402	Constitutional monarchy .... A	Luxembourg	French, Luxembourgish, German
Macao	6.6	380,000	57,576	Chinese territory under Portuguese administration C	Macao	Portuguese, Chinese (Cantonese)
† Macedonia	9,928	2,198,000	221	Republic .... A	Skopje	Macedonian, Albanian
† Madagascar	226,658	13,110,000	58	Republic .... A	Antananarivo	Malagasy, French
Maine	35,387	1,245,000	35	State (U.S.) .... D	Augusta	English
† Malawi	45,747	8,942,000	195	Republic .... A	Lilongwe	Chichewa, English
† Malaysia	127,320	19,060,000	150	Federal constitutional monarchy .... A	Kuala Lumpur	Malay, Chinese dialects, English, Tamil
† Maldives	115	246,000	2,139	Republic .... A	Male	Divehi
† Mali	482,077	8,922,000	19	Republic .... A	Bamako	French, Bambara, indigenous
† Malta	122	365,000	2,992	Republic .... A	Valletta	English, Maltese
Manitoba	250,947	1,118,000	4.5	Province (Canada) .... D	Winnipeg	English
† Marshall Islands	70	52,000	743	Republic (U.S. protection) .... A	Majuro (island)	English, indigenous, Japanese
Martinique	425	377,000	887	Overseas department (France) C	Fort-de-France	French, Creole
Maryland	12,407	5,006,000	403	State (U.S.) .... D	Annapolis	English
Massachusetts	10,555	6,106,000	578	State (U.S.) .... D	Boston	English
† Mauritania	395,956	2,142,000	5.4	Republic .... A	Nouakchott	Arabic, Pular, Soninke, Wolof
† Mauritius (incl. Dependencies)	788	1,110,000	1,409	Republic .... A	Port Louis	English, Creole, Bhojpuri, French, Hindi, Tamil, others
Mayotte (5)	144	91,000	632	Territorial collectivity (France) C	Dzaoudzi and Mamoudzou (4)	French, Swahili (Mahorian)
† Mexico	759,534	90,870,000	120	Federal republic .... A	Mexico City (Ciudad de México)	Spanish, indigenous
Michigan	96,810	9,550,000	99	State (U.S.) .... D	Lansing	English
† Micronesia, Federated States of	271	119,000	439	Republic (U.S. protection) .... A	Kolonia and Paliker (4)	English, indigenous
Midway Islands	2.0	500	250	Unincorporated territory (U.S.) C		English
Minnesota	86,943	4,539,000	52	State (U.S.) .... D	St. Paul	English
Mississippi	48,434	2,646,000	55	State (U.S.) .... D	Jackson	English
Missouri	69,709	5,266,000	76	State (U.S.) .... D	Jefferson City	English
† Moldova	13,012	4,425,000	340	Republic .... A	Chişinău (Kishinev)	Romanian (Moldovan), Russian
† Monaco	0.7	31,000	44,286	Constitutional monarchy .... A	Monaco	French, English, Italian, Monegasque
† Mongolia	604,829	2,314,000	3.8	Republic .... A	Ulan Bator (Ulaanbaatar)	Khalkha Mongol, Turkish dialects, Russian, Chinese
Montana	147,046	830,000	5.6	State (U.S.) .... D	Helena	English
Montserrat	39	13,000	333	Dependent territory (U.K.) C	Plymouth	English
† Morocco (excl. Western Sahara)	172,414	28,095,000	163	Constitutional monarchy .... A	Rabat	Arabic, Berber dialects, French
† Mozambique	308,642	16,585,000	54	Republic .... A	Maputo	Portuguese, indigenous
† Myanmar (Burma)	261,228	43,630,000	167	Provisional military government .... A	Yangon (Rangoon)	Burmese, indigenous
† Namibia	318,253	1,555,000	4.9	Republic .... A	Windhoek	English, Afrikaans, German, indigenous
Nauru	8.1	10,000	1,235	Republic .... A	Yaren District	Nauruan, English
Nebraska	77,358	1,635,000	21	State (U.S.) .... D	Lincoln	English
Nei Monggol (Inner Mongolia)	456,759	22,495,000	49	Autonomous region (China) .... D	Hohhot	Mongolian
† Nepal	56,827	20,660,000	364	Constitutional monarchy .... A	Kathmandu	Nepali, Maithali, Bhojpuri, other indigenous
† Netherlands	16,164	15,320,000	948	Constitutional monarchy .... A	Amsterdam and The Hague ('s-Gravenhage)	Dutch
Netherlands Antilles	309	192,000	621	Self-governing territory (Netherlands protection) .... B	Willemstad	Dutch, Papiamento, English
Nevada	110,567	1,375,000	12	State (U.S.) .... D	Carson City	English
New Brunswick	28,355	755,000	27	Province (Canada) .... D	Fredericton	English, French
New Caledonia	7,358	179,000	24	Overseas territory (France) C	Nouméa	French, indigenous
Newfoundland	156,649	587,000	3.7	Province (Canada) .... D	St. John's	English
New Hampshire	9,351	1,167,000	125	State (U.S.) .... D	Concord	English
New Hebrides see Vanuatu	....	....		....		
New Jersey	8,722	7,915,000	907	State (U.S.) .... D	Trenton	English
New Mexico	121,598	1,608,000	13	State (U.S.) .... D	Santa Fe	English, Spanish
New South Wales	309,500	6,117,000	20	State (Australia) .... D	Sydney	English
New York	54,475	18,375,000	337	State (U.S.) .... D	Albany	English
† New Zealand	104,454	3,486,000	33	Parliamentary state .... A	Wellington	English, Maori

Region or Political Division	Area Sq. Mi.	Est. Pop. 1/1/94	Pop. Per. Sq. Mi.	Form of Government and Ruling Power	Capital	Predominant Languages
† Nicaragua	50,054	4,267,000	85	Republic ... A	Managua	Spanish, English, indigenous
† Niger	489,191	8,754,000	18	Provisional military government ... A	Niamey	French, Hausa, Djerma, indigenous
† Nigeria	356,669	94,550,000	265	Provisional military government ... A	Lagos and Abuja	English, Hausa, Fulani, Yorbua, Ibo, indigenous
Ningxia Huizu	25,637	4,855,000	189	Autonomous region (China) ... D	Yinchuan	Chinese (Mandarin)
Niue	100	1,900	19	Self-governing territory (New Zealand protection) ... B	Alofi	English, indigenous
Norfolk Island	14	2,700	193	External territory (Australia) ... C	Kingston	English, Norfolk
North America	9,500,000	444,600,000	47			
North Carolina	53,821	6,955,000	129	State (U.S.) ... D	Raleigh	English
North Dakota	70,704	632,000	8.9	State (U.S.) ... D	Bismarck	English
Northern Ireland	5,461	1,605,000	294	Administrative division (U.K.) ... D	Belfast	English
Northern Mariana Islands	184	49,000	266	Commonwealth (U.S. protection) ... B	Saipan (island)	English, Chamorro, Carolinian
Northern Territory	519,771	172,000	0.3	Territory (Australia) ... D	Darwin	English, indigenous
Northwest Territories	1,322,910	56,000	0.1	Territory (Canada) ... D	Yellowknife	English, indigenous
† Norway (incl. Svalbard and Jan Mayen)	149,412	4,301,000	29	Constitutional monarchy ... A	Oslo	Norwegian, Lapp, Finnish
Nova Scotia	21,425	922,000	43	Province (Canada) ... D	Halifax	English
Oceania (incl. Australia)	3,300,000	28,000,000	8.5			
Ohio	44,828	11,155,000	249	State (U.S.) ... D	Columbus	English
Oklahoma	69,903	3,242,000	46	State (U.S.) ... D	Oklahoma City	English
† Oman	82,030	1,659,000	20	Monarchy ... A	Muscat	Arabic, English, Baluchi, Urdu, Indian dialects
Ontario	412,581	10,315,000	25	Province (Canada) ... D	Toronto	English
Oregon	98,386	3,009,000	31	State (U.S.) ... D	Salem	English
† Pakistan (incl. part of Jammu and Kashmir)	339,732	126,090,000	371	Federal Islamic republic ... A	Islāmābād	English, Urdu, Punjabi, Sindhi, Pashto
Palau (Belau)	196	16,000	82	Republic ... A	Koror and Melekeok (4)	Angaur, English, Japanese, Palauan, Sonsorolese, Tobi
† Panama	29,157	2,592,000	89	Republic ... A	Panamá	Spanish, English
† Papua New Guinea	178,704	3,989,000	22	Parliamentary state ... A	Port Moresby	English, Motu, Pidgin, indigenous
† Paraguay	157,048	4,297,000	27	Republic ... A	Asunción	Spanish, Guarani
Pennsylvania	46,058	12,145,000	264	State (U.S.) ... D	Harrisburg	English
† Peru	496,225	23,305,000	47	Republic ... A	Lima	Quechua, Spanish, Aymara
† Philippines	115,831	66,190,000	571	Republic ... A	Manila	English, Pilipino, Tagalog
Pitcairn (incl. Dependencies)	19	100	5.3	Dependent territory (U.K.) ... C	Adamstown	English, Tahitian
† Poland	121,196	38,540,000	318	Republic ... A	Warsaw (Warszawa)	Polish
† Portugal	35,516	9,961,000	280	Republic ... A	Lisbon (Lisboa)	Portuguese
Prince Edward Island	2,185	140,000	64	Province (Canada) ... D	Charlottetown	English
Puerto Rico	3,515	3,801,000	1,081	Commonwealth (U.S. protection) ... B	San Juan	Spanish, English
† Qatar	4,412	502,000	114	Monarchy ... A	Doha	Arabic, English
Qinghai	277,994	4,618,000	17	Province (China) ... D	Xining	Tibetan dialects, Mongolian, Turkish dialects, Chinese (Mandarin)
Quebec	594,860	7,070,000	12	Province (Canada) ... D	Québec	French, English
Queensland	666,876	3,111,000	4.7	State (Australia) ... D	Brisbane	English
Reunion	969	643,000	664	Overseas department (France) ... C	Saint-Denis	French, Creole
Rhode Island	1,545	1,012,000	655	State (U.S.) ... D	Providence	English
Rhodesia see Zimbabwe						
† Romania	91,699	22,770,000	248	Republic ... A	Bucharest (Bucureşti)	Romanian, Hungarian, German
† Russia	6,592,849	150,500,000	23	Federal republic ... A	Moscow (Moskva)	Russian, Tatar, Ukrainian
† Rwanda	10,169	8,196,000	806	Republic ... A	Kigali	French, Kinyarwanda, Kiswahili
St. Helena (incl. Dependencies)	121	7,000	58	Dependent territory (U.K.) ... C	Jamestown	English
† St. Kitts and Nevis	104	45,000	433	Parliamentary state ... A	Basseterre	English
† St. Lucia	238	151,000	634	Parliamentary state ... A	Castries	English, French
St. Pierre and Miquelon	93	7,000	75	Territorial collectivity (France) ... C	Saint Pierre	French
† St. Vincent and the Grenadines	150	115,000	767	Parliamentary state ... A	Kingstown	English, French
† San Marino	24	24,000	1,000	Republic ... A	San Marino	Italian
† Sao Tome and Principe	372	125,000	336	Republic ... A	São Tomé	Portuguese, Fang
Saskatchewan	251,866	1,006,000	4.0	Province (Canada) ... D	Regina	English
† Saudi Arabia	830,000	16,585,000	20	Monarchy ... A	Riyadh (Ar Riyāḍ)	Arabic
Scotland	30,421	5,130,000	169	Administrative division (U.K.) ... D	Edinburgh	English, Scots Gaelic
† Senegal	75,951	8,522,000	112	Republic ... A	Dakar	French, Wolof, Fulani, Serer, indigenous
† Seychelles	175	72,000	411	Republic ... A	Victoria	English, French, Creole
Shaanxi	79,151	34,455,000	435	Province (China) ... D	Xi'an (Sian)	Chinese (Mandarin)
Shandong	59,074	88,450,000	1,497	Province (China) ... D	Jinan	Chinese (Mandarin)
Shanghai	2,394	13,970,000	5,835	Autonomous city (China) ... D	Shanghai	Chinese (Wu)
Shanxi	60,232	30,075,000	499	Province (China) ... D	Taiyuan	Chinese (Mandarin)
Sichuan	220,078	112,250,000	510	Province (China) ... D	Chengdu	Chinese (Mandarin), Tibetan dialects, Miao-Yao
† Sierra Leone	27,925	4,538,000	163	Transitional military government ... A	Freetown	English, Krio, Mende, Temne, indigenous
† Singapore	246	2,834,000	11,520	Republic ... A	Singapore	Chinese (Mandarin), English, Malay, Tamil
† Slovakia	18,933	5,342,000	282	Republic ... A	Bratislava	Slovak, Hungarian
† Slovenia	7,820	1,986,000	254	Republic ... A	Ljubljana	Slovenian, Serbo-Croatian
† Solomon Islands	10,954	376,000	34	Parliamentary state ... A	Honiara	English, indigenous
† Somalia	246,201	6,541,000	27	None ... A	Mogadishu (Muqdisho)	Arabic, Somali, English, Italian
† South Africa	471,010	42,320,000	90	Republic ... A	Pretoria, Cape Town, and Bloemfontein	Afrikaans, English, Xhosa, Zulu, other indigenous
South America	6,900,000	304,500,000	44			
South Australia	379,925	1,495,000	3.9	State (Australia) ... D	Adelaide	English
South Carolina	32,007	3,657,000	114	State (U.S.) ... D	Columbia	English
South Dakota	77,121	726,000	9.4	State (U.S.) ... D	Pierre	English
South Georgia (incl. Dependencies)	1,450	(1)		Dependent territory (U.K.) ... C	Grytviken Harbour	English
South West Africa see Namibia						
† Spain	194,885	38,640,000	198	Constitutional monarchy ... A	Madrid	Spanish (Castilian), Catalan, Galician, Basque
Spanish North Africa (6)	12	142,000	11,833	Five possessions (Spain) ... C		Spanish, Arabic, Berber dialects
Spanish Sahara see Western Sahara						
† Sri Lanka	24,962	17,970,000	720	Socialist republic ... A	Colombo and Sri Jayawardenapura	English, Sinhala, Tamil
† Sudan	967,500	28,900,000	30	Provisional military government ... A	Khartoum (Al Kharṭūm)	Arabic, Nubian and other indigenous, English
† Suriname	63,251	418,000	6.6	Republic ... A	Paramaribo	Dutch, Sranan Tongo, English, Hindustani, Javanese
† Swaziland	6,704	854,000	127	Monarchy ... A	Mbabane and Lobamba	English, siSwati
† Sweden	173,732	8,747,000	50	Constitutional monarchy ... A	Stockholm	Swedish, Lapp, Finnish

Region or Political Division	Area Sq. Mi.	Est. Pop. 1/1/94	Pop. Per. Sq. Mi.	Form of Government and Ruling Power	Capital	Predominant Languages
Switzerland	15,943	7,001,000	439	Federal republic .... A	Bern (Berne)	German, French, Italian, Romansch
† Syria	71,498	13,695,000	192	Socialist republic .... A	Damascus (Dimashq)	Arabic, Kurdish, Armenian, Aramaic, Circassian
Taiwan	13,900	20,945,000	1,507	Republic .... A	T'aipei	Chinese (Mandarin), Taiwanese (Min), Hakka
† Tajikistan	55,251	5,720,000	104	Republic .... A	Dushanbe	Tajik, Uzbek, Russian
† Tanzania	364,900	27,450,000	75	Republic .... A	Dar es Salaam and Dodoma	English, Swahili, indigenous
Tasmania	26,178	483,000	18	State (Australia) .... D	Hobart	English
Tennessee	42,146	5,058,000	120	State (U.S.) .... D	Nashville	English
Texas	268,601	17,925,000	67	State (U.S.) .... D	Austin	English, Spanish
† Thailand	198,115	58,960,000	298	Constitutional monarchy .... A	Bangkok (Krung Thep)	Thai, indigenous
Tianjin (Tientsin)	4,363	9,235,000	2,117	Autonomous city (China) .... D	Tianjin (Tientsin)	Chinese (Mandarin)
† Togo	21,925	4,142,000	189	Provisional military government .... A	Lomé	French, Ewe, Mina, Kabye, Dagomba
Tokelau	4.6	1,500	326	Island territory (New Zealand) C		English, Tokelauan
Tonga	288	104,000	361	Constitutional monarchy .... A	Nuku'alofa	Tongan, English
† Trinidad and Tobago	1,980	1,288,000	651	Republic .... A	Port of Spain	English, Hindi, French, Spanish
Tristan da Cunha	40	300	7.5	Dependency (St. Helena) C	Edinburgh	English
† Tunisia	63,170	8,605,000	136	Republic .... A	Tunis	Arabic, French
† Turkey	300,948	61,540,000	204	Republic .... A	Ankara	Turkish, Kurdish, Arabic
† Turkmenistan	188,456	3,935,000	21	Republic .... A	Ashkhabad	Turkmen, Russian, Uzbek
Turks and Caicos Islands	193	13,000	67	Dependent territory (U.K.) C	Grand Turk	English
Tuvalu	10	10,000	1,000	Parliamentary state .... A	Funafuti	Tuvaluan, English
† Uganda	93,104	18,425,000	198	Republic .... A	Kampala	English, Luganda, Swahili, indigenous
† Ukraine	233,090	52,240,000	224	Republic .... A	Kiev (Kyyiv)	Ukrainian, Russian, Romanian, Polish
† United Arab Emirates	32,278	2,692,000	83	Federation of monarchs .... A	Abū Ẓaby (Abu Dhabi)	Arabic, Farsi, English, Hindi, Urdu
† United Kingdom	94,249	57,960,000	615	Parliamentary monarchy .... A	London	English, Welsh, Scots Gaelic
† United States	3,787,425	259,390,000	68	Federal republic .... A	Washington	English, Spanish
Upper Volta see Burkina Faso	....	....				
† Uruguay	68,500	3,181,000	46	Republic .... A	Montevideo	Spanish
Utah	84,904	1,842,000	22	State (U.S.) .... D	Salt Lake City	English
† Uzbekistan	172,742	22,240,000	129	Republic .... A	Tashkent	Uzbek, Russian
† Vanuatu	4,707	160,000	34	Republic .... A	Port-Vila	Bislama, English, French
Vatican City	0.2	900	4,500	Monarchical-sacerdotal state .... A	Vatican City	Italian, Latin, other
† Venezuela	352,145	20,460,000	58	Federal republic .... A	Caracas	Spanish, Amerindian
Vermont	9,615	585,000	61	State (U.S.) .... D	Montpelier	English
Victoria	87,877	4,566,000	52	State (Australia) .... D	Melbourne	English
† Vietnam	127,428	72,080,000	566	Socialist republic .... A	Hanoi	Vietnamese, French, Chinese, English, Khmer, indigenous
Virginia	42,769	6,485,000	152	State (U.S.) .... D	Richmond	English
Virgin Islands (U.S.)	133	97,000	729	Unincorporated territory (U.S.) C	Charlotte Amalie	English, Spanish, Creole
Wake Island	3.0	300	100	Unincorporated territory (U.S.) C		English
Wales	8,015	2,905,000	362	Administrative division (U.K.) .... D	Cardiff	English, Welsh Gaelic
Wallis and Futuna	98	14,000	143	Overseas territory (France) C	Mata-Utu	French, Wallisian
Washington	71,303	5,188,000	73	State (U.S.) .... D	Olympia	English
West Bank (incl. Jericho and East Jerusalem)	2,347	1,460,000	622	Israeli territory with limited self-government		Arabic, Hebrew
Western Australia	975,101	1,703,000	1.7	State (Australia) .... D	Perth	English
Western Sahara	102,703	208,000	2.0	Occupied by Morocco C		Arabic
† Western Samoa	1,093	168,000	154	Constitutional monarchy .... A	Apia	English, Samoan
West Virginia	24,231	1,816,000	75	State (U.S.) .... D	Charleston	English
Wisconsin	65,503	5,058,000	77	State (U.S.) .... D	Madison	English
Wyoming	97,818	467,000	4.8	State (U.S.) .... D	Cheyenne	English
Xinjiang Uygur (Sinkiang)	617,764	15,865,000	26	Autonomous region (China) .... D	Ürümqi	Turkish dialects, Mongolian, Tungus, English
Xizang (Tibet)	471,045	2,250,000	4.8	Autonomous region (China) .... D	Lhasa	Tibetan dialects
† Yemen	203,850	10,840,000	53	Republic .... A	Ṣan'a'	Arabic
Yugoslavia	39,449	10,730,000	272	Republic .... A	Belgrade (Beograd)	Serbo-Croatian 95%, Albanian 5%
Yukon Territory	186,661	28,000	0.2	Territory (Canada) .... D	Whitehorse	English, Inuktitut, indigenous
Yunnan	152,124	38,720,000	255	Province (China) .... D	Kunming	Chinese (Mandarin), Tibetan dialects, Khmer, Miao-Yao
† Zaire	905,446	41,675,000	46	Republic .... A	Kinshasa	French, Kikongo, Lingala, Swahili, Tshiluba, Kingwana
† Zambia	290,586	8,625,000	30	Republic .... A	Lusaka	English, Tonga, Lozi, other indigenous
Zhejiang	39,305	43,455,000	1,106	Province (China) .... D	Hangzhou	Chinese dialects
† Zimbabwe	150,873	10,605,000	70	Republic .... A	Harare (Salisbury)	English, Shona, Sindebele
WORLD	57,900,000	5,556,000,000	96	....		

† *Member of the United Nations*
. . . *None, or not applicable.*
(1) No permanent population.
(2) North Cyprus unilaterally declared its independence from Cyprus in 1983.
(3) Claimed by Argentina.
(4) Future capital.
(5) Claimed by Comoros.
(6) Comprises Ceuta, Melilla, and several small islands.

Map Symbols

In a very real sense, the whole map is a symbol, representing the world or a part of it. It is a reduced representation of the earth; each of the world's features–cities rivers, etc.–is represented on the map by a symbol. Map symbols may take the form of points, such as dots or squares (often used for cities, capital cities, or points of interest), or lines (roads, railroads, rivers). Symbols may also occupy an area, showing extent of coverage (terrain, forests, deserts). They seldom look like the feature they represent and therefore must be identified and interpreted. For instance, the maps in this atlas define political units by colored tints. Neither the colors nor the boundary lines are actually found on the surface of the earth, but because countries and states are such important political components of the world, strong symbols are used to represent them. On the maps in this atlas the surface configuration of the earth is represented by hill-shading, which gives the three-dimensional impression of landforms. This terrain representation conveys a realistic and readily visualized impression of the surface. A complete legend to the right provides a key to the other symbols on the maps in this atlas.

In this atlas a "local-name" policy generally was used for naming cities and towns and all local topographic and water features. However, for a few major cities the Anglicized name was preferred and the local name given in parentheses, for instance, Moscow (Moskva), Vienna (Wien), Prague (Praha). In countries where more than one official language is used, a name is in the dominant local language. The generic parts of local names for topographic and water features are self-explanatory in many cases because of the associated map symbols or type styles.

Cultural Features

Political Boundaries

International

Secondary: State, Provincial, etc. (Second order political unit)

Disputed de jure

Cities, Towns and Villages
(Note: On maps at 1:45,000,000 and smaller the town symbols do not follow the specific population classification shown below.

PARIS — 1,000,000 and over

Milwaukee — 250,000 to 1,000,000

Huntsville — 100,000 to 250,000

Bloomington — 25,000 to 100,000

New Meadows — 0 to 25,000

BUDAPEST — National Capitals

Springfield — Secondary Capitals

Other Cultural Features

Research Stations

Ruins

Transportation

Primary Roads

Secondary Roads

Railroads

Topographic Features

Nev. Sajama 21,463 — Peaks
Elevations are given in feet

Water Features

Lakes and Reservoirs

Fresh Water

Fresh Water: Intermittent

Salt Water

Other Water Features

Rivers

Rivers: Intermittent

Reefs

Ice Shelf

ARCTIC OCEAN

Baffin
Bay

GREENLAND
(Den.)

JAN
(No)

75°

ALASKA
(U.S.)

Anchorage

Dawson

Juneau

ICELAND

Reykjavik

FAER
(D

60°

NORTH

CANADA

Hudson
Bay

UNITED
KINGDOM

Edmonton

C

IRELAND

45°

Vancouver

Winnipeg

Seattle

Montréal

NEWFOUNDLAND

St. John's

AMERICA

Detroit
Ottawa

D

Chicago

San Francisco

UNITED STATES

Washington

New York

AZORES
(Port.)

PORTUGAL

M
SP

Los Angeles

GIBRALTAR
(U.K.)

MOROCCO

30°

Atlanta

Houston

CANARY ISLANDS
(Sp.)

ATLANTIC

W. SAHARA

MIDWAY IS.
(U.S.)

New Orleans

E

Tropic of Cancer

MEXICO

Gulf of Mexico

Havana

BAHAMAS

MAURITANIA

M

HAWAIIAN ISLANDS
(U.S.)

CUBA

DOM. REP.

CAPE VERDE

15°

Mexico City

Veracruz

HAITI

PUERTO RICO (U.S.)

SENEGAL

Dakar

BELIZE

JAMAICA

GUADELOUPE (Fr.)

GAMBIA

BU

PACIFIC

GUAT.

HOND.

MARTINIQUE (Fr.)

Caribbean
Sea

BARBADOS

GUINEA-BISSAU GUINEA

SL

EL SAL.

NIC.

F

COSTA
RICA

Caracas

TRINIDAD AND TOBAGO

SIERRA LEONE

PALMYRA
(U.S.)

PANAMA

VENEZUELA

GUYANA

Georgetown

COTE
D'IVOIRE

SURINAME

LIBERIA

COLOMBIA

Bogotá

FRENCH GUIANA

0°

Equator

GALAPAGOS ISLANDS
(Ecua.)

Quito

Belém

KIRIBATI

ECUADOR

Manaus

Fortaleza

G

SOUTH

BRAZIL

Recife

MARQUESAS IS.
(Fr.)

PERU

AMERICA

WESTERN
SAMOA

Lima

OCEAN

Salvador

OCEAN

15°

AMERICAN
SAMOA

La Paz

ST. HE
(U.

TONGA

COOK
ISLANDS
(N.Z.)

TAHITI

BOLIVIA

Brasília

Sucre

H

Tropic of Capricorn

FRENCH POLYNESIA

PARAGUAY

Rio de Janeiro

EASTER ISLAND
(Chile)

Antofagasta

São Paulo

30°

Valparaíso

ARGENTINA

URUGUAY

ARCH. DE JUAN
FERNÁNDEZ
(Chile)

Santiago

Buenos
Aires

Montevideo

I

CHATHAM IS.
(N.Z.)

45°

FALKLAND IS.
(U.K.)

SOUTH GEORGIA
(U.K.)

J

TIERRA DEL FUEGO

Punta Arenas

SOUTH SANDWICH IS.
(U.K.)

SOUTH ORKNEY IS.
(U.K.)

60°

SOUTH SHETLAND IS.
(U.K.)

Antarctic Circle

K

Weddell
Sea

Scale 1:100,000,000; one inch to 1578 miles
Robinson Projection

75°

| 0 | 400 | 800 | 1200 | 1600 | 2000 Miles |

| 0 | 600 | 1200 | 1800 | 2400 | 3000 Kilometers |

L

ARCTIC OCEAN

3   15°   14   30°   15   45°   16   60°   17   75°   18   90°   19   105°   20   120°   21   135°   22   150°   23   165°   24   180°

A

75°

SVALBARD
(Norway)

ZEMLYA FRANTSA
IOSIFA

NOVAYA
ZEMLYA

B

60°

BERING SEA

NORWAY   FINLAND   St. Petersburg
SWEDEN   Oslo
DEN.   EST.
LAT.
LITH.
GERMANY   Berlin   Warsaw   BELARUS
POLAND   Kiev   UKRAINE
MOLD.

R   U   S   S   I   A

Moscow

Novosibirsk

Irkutsk

Ulan Bator

Okhotsk

Sea of Okhotsk

SAKHALIN

C

HUNG.   BOS.
ROM.
ITALY   Rome   BULG.   Black Sea   GEO.   ARM. AZER.
ALB.   GREECE   Istanbul   TURKEY   Caspian Sea
Athens   Ankara
Algiers   TUNISIA   CRETE   CYPRUS   LEB.   SYRIA
ISRAEL   JORDAN

EUROPE

K A Z A K H S T A N

A S I A

UZBEKISTAN   KYRG.
TURKMENISTAN   TAJIK.

M O N G O L I A

Beijing

Vladivostok   HOKKAIDŌ
HONSHŪ
Sea of Japan   JAPAN
NORTH KOREA
Seoul   SOUTH KOREA   Tōkyō

45°

D

Tripoli   Cairo
LIBYA   EGYPT

IRAQ
Baghdad
Tehrān   Kābul   AFGHANISTAN
IRAN   PAKISTAN
KUWAIT   New Delhi
QATAR
SAUDI   Riyadh
ARABIA   OMAN
Mecca

C H I N A

NEPAL

Shanghai

KYŪSHŪ

PACIFIC

30°

Tropic of Cancer

E

NIGER   CHAD   SUDAN

A F R I C A

NIGERIA   CENTRAL AFRICAN
REPUBLIC
CAMEROON
EQUATORIAL
GUINEA   GABON   CONGO
TOME   RWANDA
PRINCIPE   ZAIRE   BURUNDI
Brazzaville   Kinshasa   TANZANIA
Luanda
ANGOLA   ZAMBIA

YEMEN
Aden
DJIBOUTI
Addis
Ababa
ETHIOPIA
SOMALIA
Mogadishu

KENYA   Nairobi
Dar es Salaam

Karachi

SOCOTRA
(Yem.)

ARABIAN
SEA

LAKSHADWEEP
(INDIA)

MALDIVES

SEYCHELLES

I N D I A

Bombay

Madras
Colombo
SRI LANKA

Calcutta
BANGL.
Yangon
MYANMAR
(BURMA)   LAOS
THAILAND
Bangkok   CAMBODIA
VIETNAM
Ha Noi
MACAO
(Port.)
HAINAN
Thanh Pho
Ho Chi Minh

Bay of
Bengal

Guangzhou
HONG KONG (U.K.)

South China
Sea

Manila

TAIWAN

Darwin

PHILIPPINES

NORTHERN MARIANA
ISLANDS (U.S.)

GUAM
(U.S.)

PALAU

BRUNEI
MALAYSIA
SINGAPORE
SUMATRA
BORNEO
Jakarta
JAVA
INDONESIA
NEW GUINEA
PAPUA
NEW GUINEA

WAKE
(U.S.)

OCEAN

15°

FED. STATES OF
MICRONESIA

MARSHALL
ISLANDS

Equator   0°

SOLOMON
ISLANDS

F

G

COMOROS

MADAGASCAR

I N D I A N

COCOS
ISLANDS
(Austl.)

CORAL SEA

VANUATU
FIJI

15°

H

NAMIBIA   ZIMBABWE
BOTSWANA
Pretoria
SWAZILAND
SOUTH   Maputo
AFRICA   LESOTHO   Durban
Cape Town

MOZAMBIQUE

Antananarivo   MAURITIUS
REUNION
(Fr.)

OCEAN

AUSTRALIA

Perth

Brisbane

Sydney
Canberra
Melbourne

NEW
CALEDONIA
(Fr.)   Tropic of Capricorn

Auckland
NORTH I.
NEW ZEALAND
Wellington

30°

I

ÎLES KERGUÉLEN
(Fr.)

TASMANIA   Hobart

SOUTH I.

45°

J

60°

K

Antarctic   Circle

A N T A R C T I C A

75°

L

Copyright by Rand McNally & Co.
Made in U.S.A.
DM-510000-2A-QR1- -LT-1

3   15°   14   30°   15   45°   16   60°   17   75°   18   90°   19   105°   20   120°   21   135°   22   150°   23   165°   24   180°

Scale 1:45,000,000; one inch to 710 miles
Lambert Azimuthal, Equal Area Projection

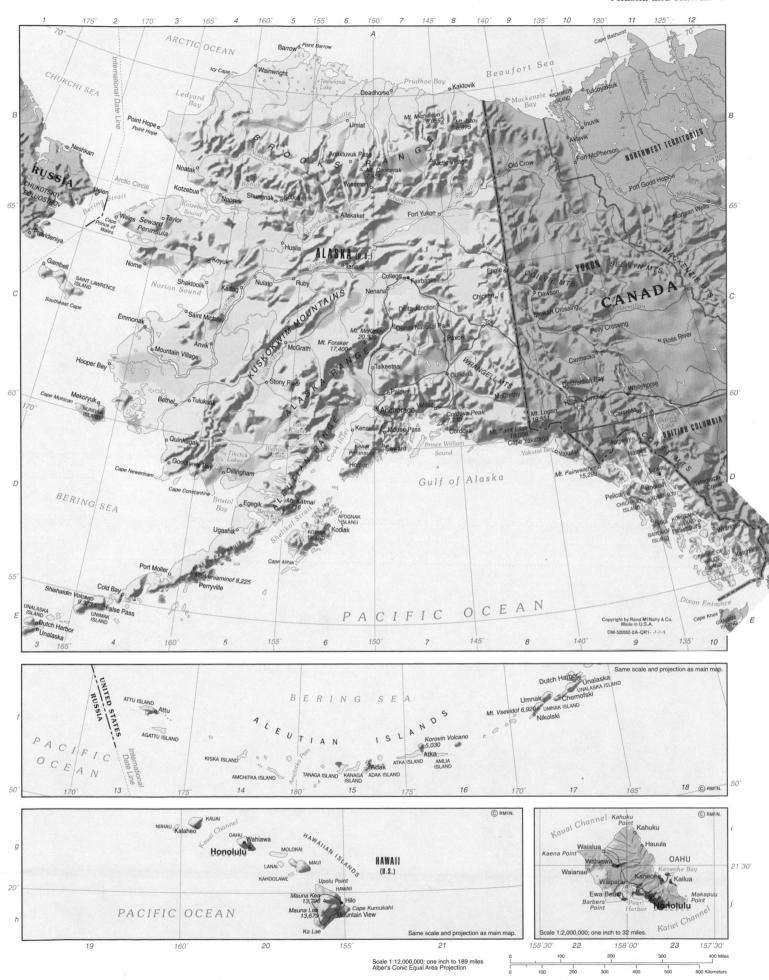

Scale 1:12,000,000; one inch to 189 miles
Alber's Conic Equal Area Projection

Scale 1:2,000,000; one inch to 32 miles.

Same scale and projection as main map.

Scale 1:16,000,000; one inch to 252 miles
Lambert Conformal Conic Projection

0 100 200 300 400 500 Miles

0 200 400 600 800 Kilometers

Scale 1:12,000,000; one inch to 189 miles
Alber's Conic Equal Area Projection

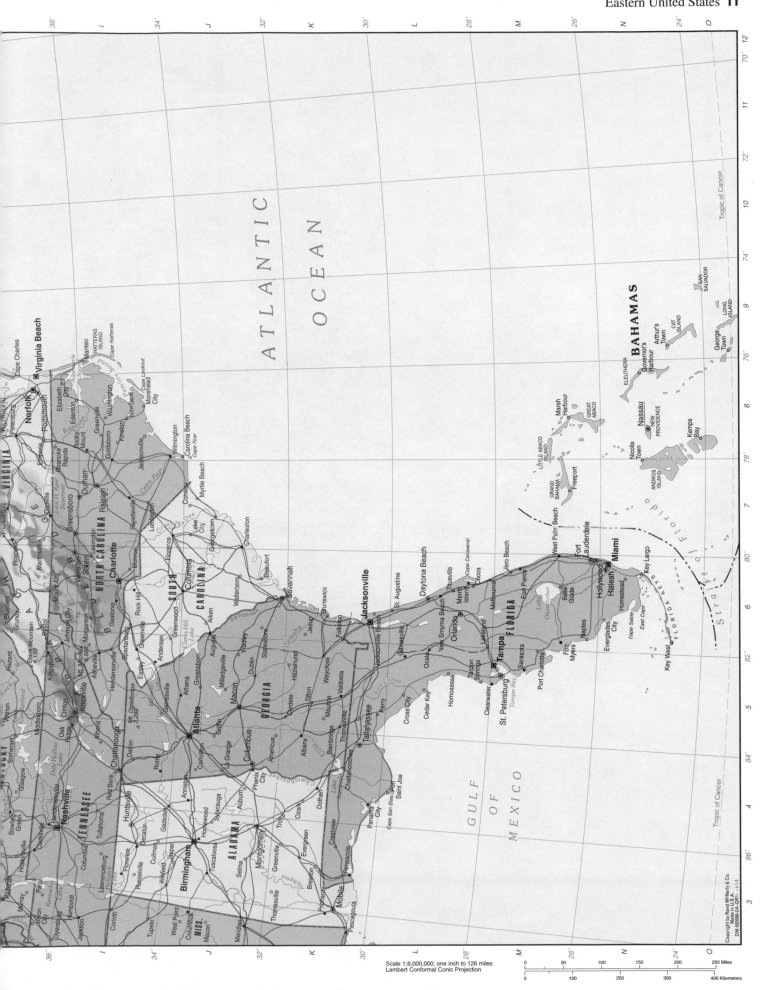

ATLANTIC

OCEAN

GULF
OF
MEXICO

BAHAMAS

Scale 1:8,000,000; one inch to 126 miles
Lambert Conformal Conic Projection

| 0 | 50 | 100 | 150 | 200 | 250 Miles |

| 0 | 100 | 200 | 300 | 400 Kilometers |

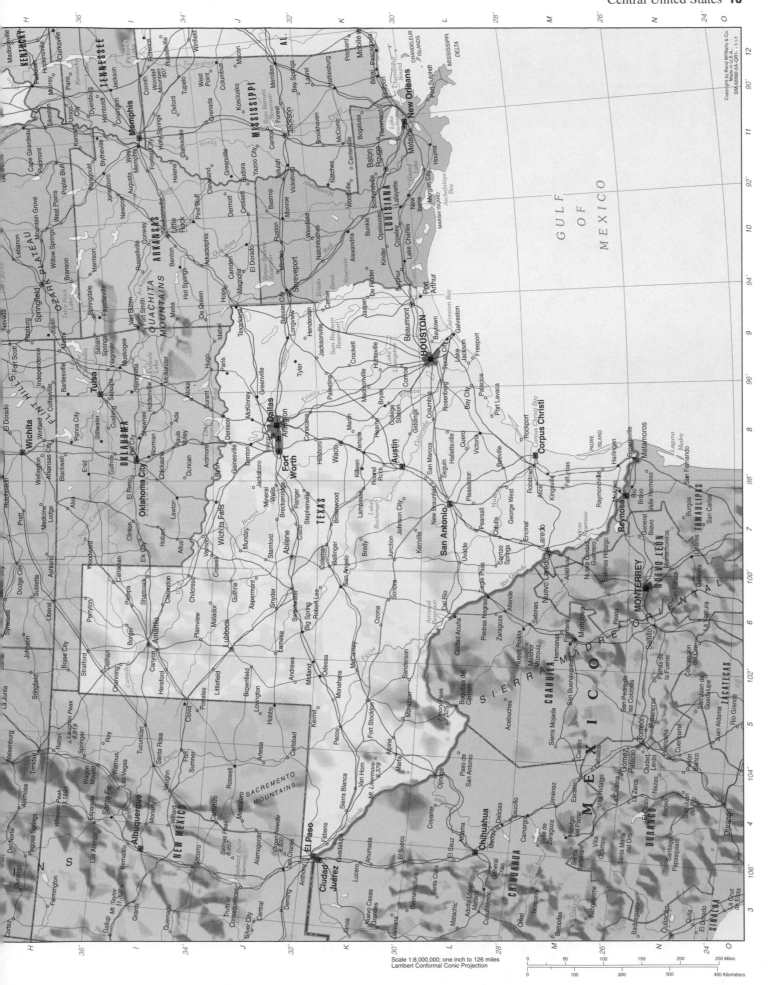

GULF
OF
MEXICO

Scale 1:8,000,000; one inch to 126 miles
Lambert Conformal Conic Projection

| 0 | 50 | 100 | 150 | 200 | 250 Miles |

| 0 | 100 | 200 | 300 | 400 Kilometers |

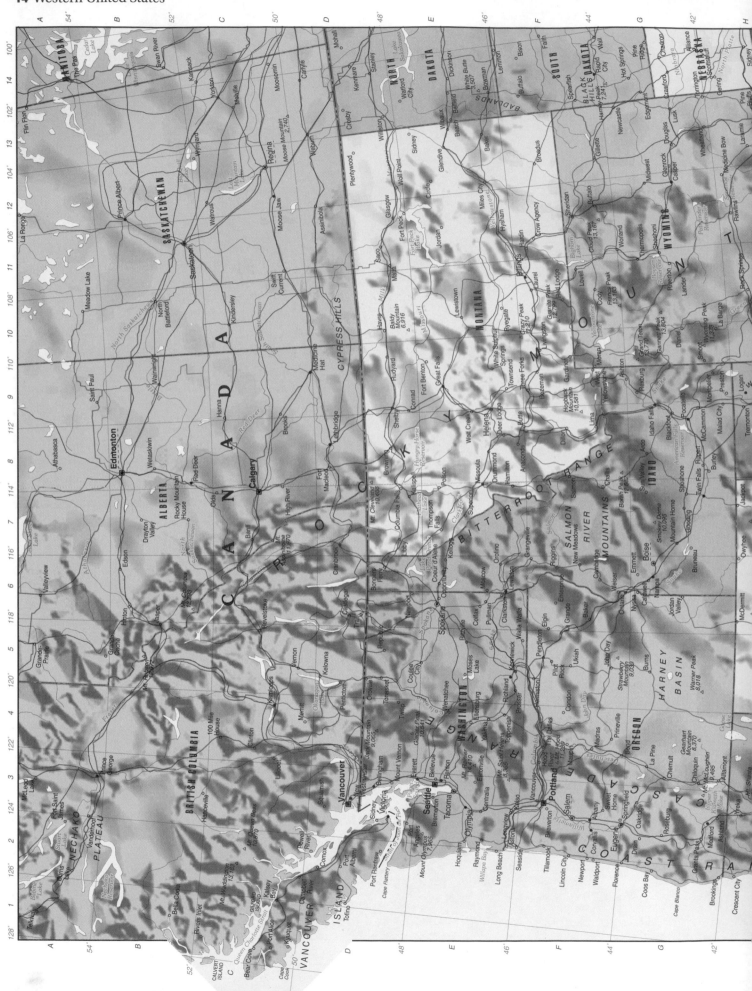

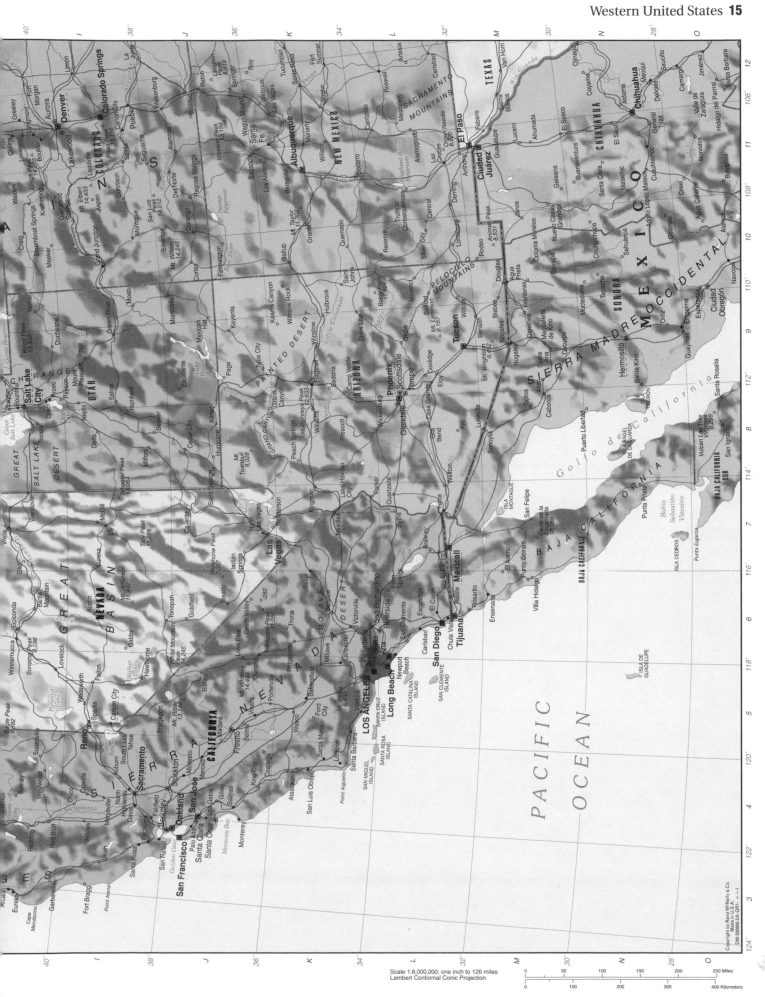

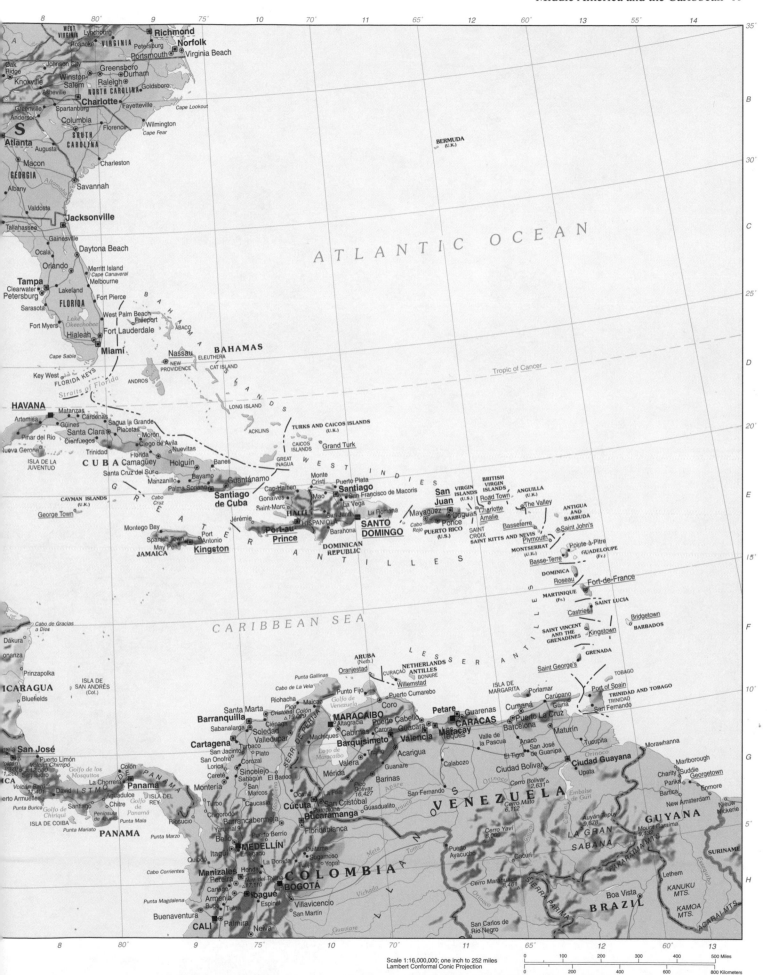

8   80°   9   75°   10   70°   11   65°   12   60°   13   55°   14   35°

WEST VIRGINIA Lynchburg, Roanoke, **Richmond**, Petersburg, Portsmouth, **Norfolk**, Virginia Beach, **VIRGINIA**

Johnson City, Greensboro, Durham, Raleigh, Goldsboro, **NORTH CAROLINA**, Winston Salem, Cape Lookout

Oak Ridge, Knoxville, Asheville, Spartanburg, **Charlotte**, Fayetteville, Cape Fear, Wilmington

Greenville, Anderson, Columbia, **SOUTH CAROLINA**, Florence, Cape Fear

Atlanta, Augusta, Charleston

GEORGIA, Macon, Savannah, BERMUDA (U.K.)

Albany, Valdosta, Jacksonville

Tallahassee, Gainesville, Daytona Beach

Ocala, Orlando, Merritt Island, Cape Canaveral, Melbourne

Tampa, Clearwater, St. Petersburg, Lakeland, Fort Pierce, **FLORIDA**, Sarasota, West Palm Beach, Freeport

Fort Myers, Lake Okeechobee, Fort Lauderdale, **Miami**, Hialeah, **BAHAMAS**

Cape Sable, Key West, FLORIDA KEYS, Nassau, NEW PROVIDENCE, ELEUTHERA, CAT ISLAND, Tropic of Cancer

ATLANTIC OCEAN

Straits of Florida, ANDROS, LONG ISLAND

HAVANA, Matanzas, Cárdenas, Sagua la Grande, Placetas, Morón, ACKLINS, CAICOS ISLANDS, TURKS AND CAICOS ISLANDS (U.K.)

Artemisa, Güines, Santa Clara, Cienfuegos, Ciego de Ávila, Grand Turk

Pinar del Río, Nueva Gerona, Trinidad, Florida, Nuevitas, GREAT INAGUA

ISLA DE LA JUVENTUD, **CUBA**, Camagüey, Holguín, Banes

Santa Cruz del Sur, Manzanillo, Bayamo, Guantánamo, Monte Cristi, Puerto Plata, **Santiago**, San Francisco de Macoris, San Juan, VIRGIN ISLANDS, BRITISH VIRGIN ISLANDS, Road Town, ANGUILLA (U.K.)

CAYMAN ISLANDS (U.K.), Cabo Cruz, Palma Soriano, **Santiago de Cuba**, Cap-Haitien, Gonaïves, Mao, La Vega, San Juan, **HAITI**, **San Juan**, Charlotte Amalie, The Valley, ANTIGUA AND BARBUDA

George Town, Montego Bay, Spanish Town, May Pen, **Kingston**, **JAMAICA**, Jérémie, Saint-Marc, **Port-au-Prince**, HISPANIOLA, Barahona, Cabo Rojo, **SANTO DOMINGO**, Mayagüez, Ponce, PUERTO RICO (U.S.), Aguas, SAINT CROIX, Basseterre, SAINT KITTS AND NEVIS, MONTSERRAT (U.K.), Plymouth, Basse-Terre, Saint John's, Pointe-à-Pitre, GUADELOUPE (Fr.)

Port Antonio, DOMINICAN REPUBLIC, DOMINICA, Roseau, Fort-de-France, MARTINIQUE (Fr.), Castries, SAINT LUCIA

CARIBBEAN SEA, SAINT VINCENT AND THE GRENADINES, Kingstown, BARBADOS, Bridgetown

Cabo de Gracias a Dios, Dákura, Prinzapolka, GRENADA, Saint George's, TOBAGO, Port of Spain, TRINIDAD AND TOBAGO

NICARAGUA, Bluefields, ISLA DE SAN ANDRÉS (Col.), ARUBA (Neth.), Oranjestad, NETHERLANDS ANTILLES, CURAÇAO, BONAIRE, Willemstad, ISLA DE MARGARITA, Porlamar, Carúpano, Güiria, San Fernando

Punta Gallinas, Cabo de La Vela, Punto Fijo, Puerto Cumarebo, Coro, Petare, Guarenas, Cumaná, Puerto La Cruz

Riohacha, Maicao, Golfo de Venezuela, **MARACAIBO**, Puerto Cabello, **CARACAS**, Barcelona, Maturín

Santa Marta, Ciénaga, Altagracia, Cabimas, Carora, Guacara, Maracay, Valle de la Pascua, Anaco, San José de Guanipa, Tucupita

Barranquilla, Sabanalarga, Soledad, Machiques, Valencia, Acarigua, El Tigre, Ciudad Guayana

Cartagena, San Jacinto, Turbaco, Corozal, Lara, Valera, Guanare, Calabozo, Ciudad Bolívar, Upata, Morawhanna

San Onofre, Sincelejo, El Banco, Trujillo, Barinas, Cerro Bolívar 2,631, Marlborough, Charity, Suddie, Georgetown

Lorica, Cereté, Sahagún, San Marcos, **Mérida**, Parika, Bartica, Enmore

San José, Puerto Limón, Volcán Chirripó, Monteria, Caucasia, Ocaña, La Fría, San Fernando, Cerro Yaví 8,069, New Amsterdam, Nieuw Nickerie

Panamá, Chitré, ISLA DEL REY, Turbo, Chigorodo, Barrancabermeja, Cúcuta, **Bucaramanga**, Guasdualito, **VENEZUELA**, Cerro Mato 6,112, **GUYANA**, SURINAME

Golfo de Montijo, Golfo de San Miguel, Yarumal, Bello, Floridablanca, Auyán Tepuy 2,631, LA GRAN SABANA, Mount Roraima 9,438, Lethem

ISTMO DE PANAMÁ, **MEDELLÍN**, Itagüí, Buenaventura, La Dorada, Duitama, Sogamoso, Yopal, Puerto Ayacucho, Cacurí, KANUKU MTS., KAMOA MTS.

Manizales, Pereira, Armenia, **Ibagué**, Espinal, Villavicencio, San Martín, **BOGOTÁ**, **BRAZIL**, Boa Vista, PAKARAIMA MTS., ACARAI MTS.

Buenaventura, Buga, Tuluá, Palmira, Neiva, Guaviare, San Carlos de Río Negro, **COLOMBIA**, **CALI**

8   80°   9   75°   10   70°   11   65°   12   60°   13

Scale 1:16,000,000; one inch to 252 miles
Lambert Conformal Conic Projection

0   100   200   300   400   500 Miles

0   200   400   600   800 Kilometers

PACIFIC OCEAN

GULF OF MEXICO

Scale 1:8,000,000; one inch to 126 miles
Lambert Conformal Conic Projection

GULF OF MEXICO

U.S.

Cape Sable ⊙ **Miami**

Mérida

YUCATAN PENINSULA

Canal de Yucatán

BAHAMAS

Tropic of Cancer

ATLANTIC OCEAN

HAVANA ■

CUBA

MEXICO

GUATEMALA

Belmopan BELIZE

Gulf of Honduras

HONDURAS

HAITI

DOMINICAN REPUBLIC

PUERTO RICO (U.S.)

Santo DOMINGO

LESSER ANTILLES

GUADELOUPE (Fr.)

JAMAICA

Kingston

Port-au-Prince

SAINT LUCIA

GUATEMALA ■

San Salvador ⊙

EL SALVADOR

Tegucigalpa

NICARAGUA

Lago de Nicaragua

CARIBBEAN SEA

TRINIDAD AND TOBAGO

San José ⊙

Managua ⊙

COSTA RICA

Panama ■

PANAMA

Golfo de Panamá

Punta Gallinas

Barranquilla

Cartagena

MARACAIBO

CARACAS ■

Barquisimeto

Boca Grande

Cúcuta

Palmarito

LLANOS

Orinoco

Georgetown ⊙

MEDELLÍN

Nev. del Tolima 17,110

Bucaramanga

VENEZUELA

GUYANA

Cacurí

Paramaribo ⊙

Cayenne ⊙

Cabo Caciporé

BOGOTÁ ■

CALI

COLOMBIA

SURINAME

PAKARAIMA

Boa Vista

FRENCH GUIANA

Punta Magdalena

Nev. del Huila 18,865

Lérida

San Carlos de Río Negro

Cabo Norte

Punta Galera

Taraquá

QUITO ■

Cayambe 18,996

ECUADOR

Equator

GALÁPAGOS ISLANDS (Ec.)

Japurá

MACAPÁ

Ilha de Marajó

Baía de Marajó

Equator

Putumayo

MANAUS

Santarém

Iquitos

Tamaniqué

Belém

São Luís

ECUADOR ■

GUAYAQUIL

Punta Pariñas

Eirunepé

Amazon

Madeira

Juruá

Conceição

BRAZIL

Imperatriz

Fortaleza

ILHA FERNANDO DE NORONHA

Teresina

Cabo de São Roque

Chiclayo

P E R U

Putumayo

Porto Velho

Ji-Paraná

Conceição do Araguaia

Natal

RECIFE

Represa de Sobradinho

Nev. Huascarán 22,133

ANDES

Callao

Lima

Cusco

Punta Carreta

Puerto Heath

Nev. Illampu 21,066

Trinidad

Cuiabá

PLANALTO DO MATO GROSSO

Alta Floresta

Feira de Santana

Aracaju

SALVADOR

Lago Titicaca

LA PAZ ■

Goiânia

BRASÍLIA ■

Itabuna

Arequipa

Oruro

BOLIVIA

Santa Cruz de la Sierra

Sucre

SERRA DO ESPINHAÇO

Ponta da Baleia

Iquique

Nev. Sajama 21,463

Uberlândia

Represa de Três Marias

Anambaí

BELO HORIZONTE

Cabo de São Tomé

Antofagasta

GRAN CHACO

PARAGUAY

Londrina

Punta Ballenita

ISLA SAN AMBROSIO (Chile)

Nev. Ojos del Salado 22,615

A N D E S

Asunción ■

SÃO PAULO

RIO DE JANEIRO

Tropic of Capricorn

PACIFIC OCEAN

ISLA SAN FÉLIX (Chile)

Punta Cachos

San Miguel de Tucumán

Paraná

Santo André

Tropic of Capricorn

Florianópolis

Santa María

PORTO ALEGRE

ARCHIPIÉLAGO JUAN FERNÁNDEZ (Chile)

Santiago del Estero

Goya

Lagoa dos Patos

Ponta do Bojuru

Valparaíso

CHILE

Cerro Aconcagua 22,831

CÓRDOBA

ROSARIO

Santa Fe

URUGUAY

Lagoa Mirim

Santiago ⊙

ARGENTINA

BUENOS AIRES ■

MONTEVIDEO ■

Concepción

Punta Morguilla

La Plata

Punta del Este

Río de la Plata

Bahía Blanca

Valdivia

Neuquén

Mar del Plata

Cabo Quedal

Golfo San Matías

ISLA GRANDE DE CHILOÉ

Península Valdés

ATLANTIC OCEAN

ARCHIPIÉLAGO DE LOS CHONOS

PATAGONIA

Cabo dos Bahías

Golfo San Jorge

Comodoro Rivadavia

TRISTAN DA CUNHA GROUP (St. Helena)

Península de Taitao

Punta Medanoso

GOUGH ISLAND (St. Helena)

ISLA WELLINGTON

Bahía Grande

FALKLAND ISLANDS (U.K.)

WEST FALKLAND

Stanley

EAST FALKLAND

Cabo Deseado

Strait of Magellan

Punta Arenas

TIERRA DEL FUEGO

ISLA SANTA INÉS

Cape Horn (Cabo de Hornos)

SOUTH GEORGIA (U.K.)

Drake Passage

SOUTH SHETLAND ISLANDS (U.K.)

SOUTH ORKNEY ISLANDS (U.K.)

SOUTH SANDWICH ISLANDS (U.K.)

BOUVET (Nor.)

Antarctic Circle

ALEXANDER ISLAND

Antarctic Peninsula

| 0 | 200 | 400 | 600 | 800 | 1000 Miles |

| 0 | 300 | 600 | 900 | 1200 | 1500 Kilometers |

Scale 1:45,000,000; one inch to 710 miles
Lambert Azimuthal, Equal Area Projection

PACIFIC OCEAN

ATLANTIC OCEAN

BOLIVIA

PARAGUAY

BRAZIL

Tropic of Capricorn

ARGENTINA

CHILE

URUGUAY

FALKLAND ISLANDS
(U.K.)

SOUTH GEORGIA
(U.K.)

Tocopilla
Chuquicamata
Tarija
Tartagal
Antofagasta
Cerro Licancábur 19,409
Calama
San Salvador de Jujuy
Volcán Llullaillaco 22,110
Salta
Punta Dos Reyes
Cerro Galán △ 19,396
Nevado Ojos del Salado 22,615
San Miguel de Tucumán
Punta Ballenita
Copiapó
Cerro Bonete △ 22,546
Concepción
Punta Medio
Punta Cachos
Santiago del Estero
San Fernando del Valle de Catamarca
Cabo Bascuñán
La Rioja
Vallenar
Reconquista
La Serena
Cerro de las Tórtolas 20,735
Coquimbo
CÓRDOBA
Rafaela
Punta Lengua de Vaca
Ovalle
San Juan
San Francisco
Santa Fe
Alta Gracia
Río Tercero
Paraná
Cerro Aconcagua 22,831
Villa María
San Felipe
Villa Nueva
Bell-Ville
San Lorenzo
Viña del Mar
Quillota
Mendoza
San Luis
ROSARIO
Valparaíso
Villa Alemana
San Martín
Villa Constitución
Santiago
Puente Alto
San Bernardo
Mercedes
Venado Tuerto
General San Martín
San Antonio
Rancagua
Villa Dolores
Pergamino
Zárate
BUENOS AIRES
Punta Topocalma
San Fernando
Junín
Lomas de Zamora
Avellaneda
Curicó
San Rafael
Nueve de Julio
La Plata
MONTEVIDEO
Talca
Cerro el Nevado △ 12,500
Pehuajó
Linares
Santa Rosa
Chillán
Azul
Talcahuano
Tomé
Olavarría
Tandil
Concepción
Coronel
Lota
Balcarce
Mar del Plata
Los Ángeles
Tres Arroyos
Angol
Bahía Blanca
Necochea
Punta Morguilla
Temuco
Neuquén
Cipolletti
Punta Alta
General Roca
Pedro Luro
Valdivia
General Conesa
Osorno
San Antonio Oeste
Viedma
Punta Rasa
Cabo Quedal
Puerto Montt
San Carlos de Bariloche
Monte Tronador 11,453
Ancud
Castro
Puerto Madryn
Punta Delgada
Isla Grande de Chiloé
Quellón
Volcán Corcovado 7,546
Esquel
Trelew
Punta Ninfas
Rawson
José de San Martín
Puerto Aisén
Coihaique
Cabo Dos Bahías
Archipiélago de los Chonos
Sarmiento
Comodoro Rivadavia
Caleta Olivia
Parito Moreno
Fitz Roy
Cerro San Clemente 13,314
Lago Posadas
Puerto Deseado
Punta Medanosa
Isla Byron
Tamel Aike
Bahía Laura
Isla Campana
Punta Desengaño
Isla Patricio Lynch
Cerro Chaltel o Monte Fitzroy 10,958
Puerto San Julián
Isla Wellington
Isla Mornington
Puerto Santa Cruz
Bahía Grande
El Calafate
Isla Madre de Dios
Río Gallegos
Cabo Vírgenes
Isla Diego de Almagro
El Turbio
Puerto Natales
Punta Catalina
Cabo Deseado
Punta de Arenas
Isla Riesco
Isla Desolación
Punta Arenas
Porvenir
Río Grande
Isla Santa Inés
TIERRA DEL FUEGO
Cabo San Diego
Cabo San Juan
Ushuaia
ISLA DE LOS ESTADOS
Isla Navarino
Falso Cabo de Hornos
Cape Horn (Cabo de Hornos)

WEST FALKLAND
Cape Dolphin
Mount Usborne 2,312
Stanley
EAST FALKLAND
Cape Meredith
Falkland Sound

Scale 1:16,000,000; one inch to 252 miles
Lambert Conformal Conic Projection

0   100   200   300   400   500 Miles
0   200   400   600   800 Kilometers

NICARAGUA

COSTA RICA

San José

PANAMÁ
Panamá

NETHERLANDS ANTILLES
ARUBA (Neth.)
CURAÇAO   BONAIRE

Santa Marta
Barranquilla
Cartagena
MARACAIBO
Petare   Guarenas
CARACAS
Barquisimeto
Valencia   Maracay
Barcelona
Cumaná
ISLA DE MARGARITA

Cúcuta
Bucaramanga
MEDELLÍN
Manizales
Pereira
Armenia
Ibagué
BOGOTÁ
CALI
Popayán
Pasto

COLOMBIA

VENEZUELA

Ciudad Guayana
Ciudad Bolívar

ISLA DEL COCO
(Costa Rica)

ISLA DE MALPELO
(Colombia)

Esmeraldas
QUITO
ECUADOR
Manta
Portoviejo
Ambato
Chimborazo 20,702
Riobamba
GUAYAQUIL
Cuenca
Machala
Loja

SAN CRISTOBAL
GALAPAGOS ISLANDS
(ARCHIPIELAGO DE COLÓN)
(Ecuador)

Equator

Iquitos

Leticia

AMAZONAS

SELVA

Tumbes
Talara
Piura
Chiclayo
Pacasmayo
Trujillo
Chimbote
Nev. Huascarán 22,133
Huaraz

PERU

Cruzeiro do Sul
Pucallpa

ACRE
Rio Branco

RONDÔNIA
Porto Velho
Ariquemes
Ji-Paraná
Guajará-Mirim

Huánuco
Cerro de Pasco
La Oroya
Callao
Lima
Huancayo
Ayacucho
Cusco
Machupicchu

Pisco
Ica
Nazca

CORDILLERA ORIENTAL

Puerto Maldonado
Puerto Heath

Trinidad

BOLIVIA
LA PAZ
Cochabamba
Santa Cruz de la Sierra
Oruro
Sucre
Potosí

Arequipa
Volcán Misti 19,101
Moquegua
Ilo
Tacna
Arica

Puno
Lago Titicaca
Juliaca

ALTIPLANO

PACIFIC OCEAN

Iquique

ARGENTINA

CHILE

ATLANTIC OCEAN

TOBAGO
TRINIDAD AND TOBAGO
Port of Spain
San Fernando
TRINIDAD

Boca Grande

Morawhanna
Marlborough
Charity   Suddie
Parika   Georgetown
Bartica   Enmore
New Amsterdam
Nieuw
Nickerie   Groningen   Paramaribo
GUYANA   Nieuw Amsterdam   Iracoubo
Albina   Saint-Laurent-   Sinnamary
Mount Roraima 9,432   Kwakoegron   du-Maroni   Kourou
Brokopondo   Saint-Élie   Cayenne
Stuumeer   Guisanbourg

GUYANA
Boa Vista   Lethem   KANUKU   SURINAME   FRENCH   Quanary
MTS.   Juliana Top 4,035   GUIANA   Cabo Caciporé
KORAIMA   KAMOA   ACARAI MTS.   Saül
MTS.   TUMUC-HUMAC MOUNTAINS   ILHA DE MARACÁ
Cabo Norte

AMAPÁ

ILHA BAILIQUE
ILHA DO CURUÁ
ILHA JANAUCU
ILHA CAVIANA DE FORA
ILHA MEXIANA
Cabo Maguari   Equator
Macapá
ILHA   Soure
GRANDE   Baía de Marajó
DO GURUPÁ   ILHA DE   Bragança
Oriximiná   MARAJÓ   Capanema
Faro   Breves   Belém   Castanhal   Carutapera
Portel   Abaetetuba   São
MANAUS   Santarém   Pará   Cametá   Luís   Parnaíba
Manacapuru   Itacoatiara   Altamira   Camocim
Maués   Tucuruí   Pindaré Mirim   Itapipoca   Fortaleza
Itaituba   Represa de   Bacabal   Coroatá   Sobral   Maracanaú
Tucuruí   Codó   Caxias   Piripiri   Caninde   Pacajus
Novo   Marabá   Imperatriz   MARANHÃO   Timon   Campo   CEARÁ   Quixadá
Aripuanã   SERRA DOS CARAJÁS   Teresina   Maior   Crateús   Mossoró
PARÁ   Nazaré   Tocantinópolis   São João dos   Floriano   Picos   Jaguaribe   RIO GRANDE DO NORTE   Natal
Conceição   Araguaína   Patos   Igatu   Juazeiro   Caicó
da Araguaia   Carolina   Oeiras   PIAUÍ   do Norte   Patos   PARAÍBA   João
Balsas   Represa Boa   Crato   Salgueiro   Serra Talhada   Campina   Pessoa
Esperança   Palmas   Grande   Olinda
Alta Floresta   Conceição   PERNAMBUCO   Arcoverde   RECIFE
da Araguaia   Porto Nacional   Petrolina   Garanhuns   Caruaru   Palmares
BRAZIL   Juàzeiro   Pálmeira dos   ALAGOAS
MATO GROSSO   TOCANTINS   Paulo Afonso   Índios   Maceió
Gurupi   Represa de   Senhor do   Arapiraca
Sobradinho   Bonfim   SERGIPE   Penedo
Irocó   Jacobina   Aracaju
Barreiras   Esplanada
Ibotirama   BAHIA   Feira de   Alagoinhas
Santana   Itaberaba   Santana   Camaçari
Bom Jesus   SALVADOR
Cuiabá   da Lapa   Valença
PLANALTO   Porangatu   Guanambi   Jequié
DO MATO   Jaciara   Brumado   Ilhéus
GROSSO   Barra do Garças   Formosa   Ipiaú   Itabuna
Diamantino   BRASÍLIA   Januária   Vitória da   Itapetinga
DISTRITO FEDERAL   São   Conquista   Canavieiras
Luziânia   Francisco   Pedra Azul   Belmonte
Ipurá   Unaí   Montes Claros   Salinas   Itaobim
Anápolis   Paracatu   Itamaraju
Caiapônia   Goiânia   Pirapora   Almenara   Ponta da Baleia
Mineiros   GOIÁS   Pires do   João   Bocaiúva   Teófilo Otoni   Nanuque
Jataí   Rio   Pinheiro   MINAS   Curvelo
Coxim   Pontalina   GERAIS   Governador   São Mateus
Rio Verde de   Iumbiara   Patos de   Valadares
Mato Grosso   Harumá   Minas   Ipatinga   Linhares
MATO GROSSO   Uberlândia   Araguari   BELO   Colatina
DO SUL   Camapuã   Araxá   Sete Lagoas   HORIZONTE   Vitória
Campo Grande   Frutal   Uberaba   Ponte Nova   Vila Velha
Miranda   São José do   Ponte   Cachoeiro de Itapemirim
Aquidauana   Três Lagoas   Rio Preto   Franca   Pocos de Caldas   São João   Nova Friburgo   Itaguaí
Araçatuba   Ribeirão Preto   Lavras   del Rei   Campos
Bela Vista   Araraquara   Volta   RIO DE JANEIRO   Cabo de São Tomé
Dourados   Lins   Tupã   São Carlos   Redonda   Três Rios   Niterói
Pedro Juan   Marília   SÃO PAULO   Juiz de Fora
Caballero   Ponta Porã   Assis   Bauru   Campinas   Nova Iguaçu
Piracicaba   RIO DE JANEIRO
PARAGUAY   São José dos Campos   Taubaté
Sorocaba   SÃO PAULO
Santo André   Santos
São Vicente

RORAIMA
Branco
ARAN
ABANA
Esequebo
Kaieteur
Rupununi
PAKARAIMA MTS.

Represa
Balbina
Trombetas
Paru de Oeste
Mapuera
Nhamundá
Parú
AMAPÁ
Amazon
Xingu
Tapajós
Iriri
SERRA DO NORTE
SERRA DOS APIACÁS
SERRA DO CACHIMBO
SERRA DOS PARECIS
SERRA FORMOSA
SERRA DO RONCADOR
SERRA DO TOMBADOR
Araguaia
Rio das Mortes
Xingu
Tocantins
Araguaia
SERRA DO ESPINHAÇO
SERRA DAS MANGABEIRAS
CHAPADA DAS MANGABEIRAS
SERRA DO PENITENTE
SERRA DO URUÇUÍ
São Francisco
SERRA DO ESPINHAÇO
CHACO BOREAL

Scale 1:16,000,000; one inch to 252 miles
Lambert Azimuthal, Equal Area Projection
Tropic of Capricorn
10

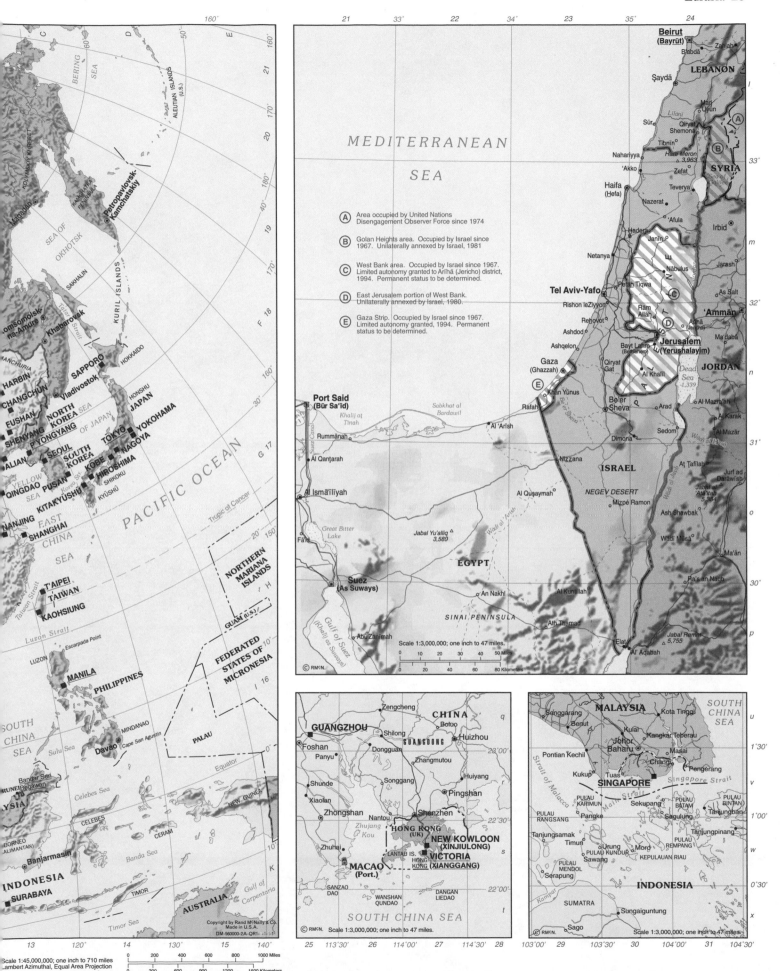

MEDITERRANEAN SEA

(A) Area occupied by United Nations Disengagement Observer Force since 1974

(B) Golan Heights area. Occupied by Israel since 1967. Unilaterally annexed by Israel, 1981

(C) West Bank area. Occupied by Israel since 1967. Limited autonomy granted to Arīḥā (Jericho) district, 1994. Permanent status to be determined.

(D) East Jerusalem portion of West Bank. Unilaterally annexed by Israel, 1980.

(E) Gaza Strip. Occupied by Israel since 1967. Limited autonomy granted, 1994. Permanent status to be determined.

Beirut (Bayrūt)
Zahlah
B'abdā
LEBANON
Şaydā
Marj 'Uyūn
Lītanī
Qiryat Shemona
Ḥare Meron △ 3,963
Sūr
Tibnīn
B
Nahariyya
'Akko
Zefat
SYRIA
Haifa (Ḥefa)
Teverya
A
Nazerat
'Afula
Irbid
Hadera
Janīn
Jarash
Netanya
Nābulus
As Salt
Petaḥ Tiqwa
'Ammān
Tel Aviv-Yafo
C
Rishon leZiyyon
Rām Allāh
Rehovot
D
Ma'dabā
Jerusalem (Yerushalayim)
Ashdod
Bayt Laḥm (Bethlehem)
Ashqelon
Qiryat Gat
Al Khalīl
Arīḥā (Jericho)
Dead Sea -1,339
JORDAN
Gaza (Ghazzah)
Be'er Sheva
E
Khān Yūnus
Al Mazra'ah
Rafaḥ
Arad
Al Karak
Sedom
Al Mazār
Port Said (Būr Sa'īd)
Sabkhat al Bardawīl
Khalīj aṭ Tīnah
Al 'Arīsh
Aṭ Ṭafīlah
Rummānah
Niẓẓana
Dimona
Jurf ad Darāwīsh
ISRAEL
Al Qanṭarah
Al Quṣaymah
NEGEV DESERT
Jabal el 'Aṭā'iṭah 5,384
Al Ismā'īlīyah
Mizpé Ramon
Great Bitter Lake
Jabal Yu'alliq △ 3,589
Wādī Mūsā
Fā'īd
Ma'ān
Ash Shawbak
EGYPT
Ra's an Naqb
Suez (As Suways)
An Nakhl
Al Kuntillah
SINAI PENINSULA
Ath Thamad
Jabal Ramm △ 5,755
Abū Zanīmah
Elat
Gulf of Suez (Khalīj as Suways)
Al 'Aqabah

Scale 1:3,000,000; one inch to 47 miles.
0   10   20   30   40   50 Miles
0   20   40   60   80 Kilometers
© RM&N.

BERING SEA
KOLYMSKIY KHREBET
ALEUTIAN ISLANDS (U.S.)
KAMCHATKA PENINSULA
Petropavlovsk-Kamchatskiy
Magadan
SEA OF OKHOTSK
Komsomol'sk-na-Amure
SAKHALIN
KURIL ISLANDS
Khabarovsk
Tatar Strait
MANCHURIA
HOKKAIDO
HARBIN
SAPPORO
CHANGCHUN
Vladivostok
FUSHUN
NORTH KOREA
SHENYANG
SEA OF JAPAN
P'YONGYANG
JAPAN
HONSHU
SEOUL
TOKYO
YOKOHAMA
DALIAN
SOUTH KOREA
KOBE
NAGOYA
QINGDAO
KITAKYUSHU
PUSAN
HIROSHIMA
YELLOW SEA
Korea St.
KYŪSHŪ
SHIKOKU
NANJING
EAST CHINA SEA
SHANGHAI
PACIFIC OCEAN
Tropic of Cancer
T'AIPEI
TAIWAN
KAOHSIUNG
Taiwan Strait
NORTHERN MARIANA ISLANDS
Luzon Strait
Escarpada Point
LUZON
GUAM (U.S.)
MANILA
PHILIPPINES
FEDERATED STATES OF MICRONESIA
SOUTH CHINA SEA
MINDANAO
Davao
Cape San Agustin
PALAU
Sulu Sea
Equator
Bandar Seri Begawan
BRUNEI
MALAYSIA
Celebes Sea
NEW GUINEA
CELEBES
CERAM
Banda Sea
BORNEO (KALIMANTAN)
Banjarmasin
INDONESIA
SURABAYA
TIMOR
Timor Sea
Gulf of Carpentaria
AUSTRALIA

Scale 1:45,000,000; one inch to 710 miles
Lambert Azimuthal, Equal Area Projection
0   200   400   600   800   1000 Miles
0   300   600   900   1200   1500 Kilometers

Zengcheng
CHINA
GUANGZHOU
Shilong
Botuo
Huizhou
Foshan
GUANGDONG
Dongguan
Panyu
Zhangmutou
Songgang
Huiyang
Shunde
Pingshan
Xiaolan
Zhongshan
Nantou
Shenzhen
Zhuhai
Zhujiang Kou
HONG KONG (UK)
NEW KOWLOON (XINJIULONG)
LANTAU IS.
VICTORIA
MACAO (Port.)
HONG KONG (XIANGGANG)
SANZAO DAO
WANSHAN QUNDAO
DANGAN LIEDAO
SOUTH CHINA SEA

© RM&N. Scale 1:3,000,000; one inch to 47 miles.

Senggarang
MALAYSIA
Kota Tinggi
SOUTH CHINA SEA
Benut
Kulai
Kangkar Teberau
Pontian Kechil
Johor Baharu
Masai
Changi
Kukup
Pengerang
Strait of Malacca
Tuas
Singapore Strait
SINGAPORE
PULAU KARIMUN
Sekupang
PULAU BATAM
PULAU BINTAN
PULAU RANGSANG
Pangke
Sagulung
Tanjungban
Tanjungsamak
PULAU KUNDUR
Urung
Moro
Tanjungpinang
Timun
Sawang
KEPULAUAN RIAU
PULAU REMPANG
PULAU MENDOL
Serapung
SUMATRA
INDONESIA
Sungaiguntung
Sago

© RM&N. Scale 1:3,000,000; one inch to 47 miles.

Scale 1:16,000,000; one inch to 252 miles
Lambert Conformal Conic Projection

ARCTIC OCEAN

Horn
Siglufjörður
GRIMSEY
Rifstangi
Fontur
Snæfellsnes
Breiðafjörður
Faxaflói
Sauðárkrókur
Akureyri
Húsavík
ICELAND
Reykjavík
Keflavík
Þingvellir
Selfoss
Hvannadalshnúkur 6,952 △
Hekla 4,892 △
Djúpivogur
Reykjanes
Vestmannaeyjar
Stokksnes

NORWEGIAN SEA

LOFOTEN VESTERÅLEN
Narvik
Kebnekaise 6,926
Bodø
Mo
Mosjøen
Namsos
Sørsele
Storuman
Vilhelmina
Steinkjer
Levanger
Åsele
Trondheim
Østersund
Sollefteå
Härnösand
Dombås
Galdhøpiggen 8,100 △
Mora
Sundsv
Ålesund
Sarna
SWEDEN
Sognafjorden
NORWAY
Lillehammer
Hamar
Hudiksv
Bollnäs
Bergen
Logen
Falun
Gävle
Borlänge
Sandviken
Haugesund
OSLO
Arvika
Uppsala
Drammen
Karlstad
Västerås
Stavanger
Skien
Sandefjord
Halden
Säffle
Örebro
STOCKHOLM
Egersund
Porsgrunn
Eskilstuna
Söderta
Arendal
Katrineholm
Nyköping
Kristiansand
Mandal
Uddevalla
Skövde
Norrköping
Lindesnes
Trollhättan
Linköping
Göteborg
Jönköping
Västervik
Visb
Skagerrak
Frederikshavn
Grenen
Borås
Vetlanda
Oskarshamn
Ålborg
Varberg
Värnamo
ÖLAND
Holstebro
Kattegat
Halmstad
Ljungby
Kalmar
Borgholm
Viborg
Randers
Fornæs
Helsingborg
Karlshamn
Kalmar
Karlskrona
DENMARK
Århus
Copenhagen
(København)
Kolding
Odense
Malmö
Trelleborg
BORNHOLM (Den.)
Esbjerg
SJÆLLAND
Rønne
BALTI
Flensburg
Næstved
Schleswig
Nykøbing
Kap Arkona
Lebork
Cuxhaven
LOLLAND
Itzehoe
Lübeck
Stralsund
Koszalin
Kołobrzeg
Gdańs
Wilhelmshaven
Kiel
Rostock
Świnoujście
Szczecinek
Chojn
Leeuwarden
Bremerhaven
Schwerin
Neubrandenburg
Szczecin
Stargard
Wałcz
Świec
NETHERLANDS
Gröningen
Oldenburg
HAMBURG
Wittenberge
Schwedt
Gerzów Wielkopolski
Bydgoszcz
Den Helder
Emden
Bremen
Hannover
GERMANY
BERLIN
Fürstenwalde
Poznań
Amsterdam
Osnabrück
Bielefeld
Hildesheim
Braunschweig
Potsdam
Cottbus
Zielona Góra
Kalisz
Haarlem
Utrecht
Münster
Magdeburg
Gnjez
Leiden
Rotterdam
Dortmund
Dessau
Poznań
The Hague
('s-Gravenhage)
Antwerpen
Essen
Wuppertal
Düsseldorf
Göttingen
Halle
Leipzig
Głogów
Brugge
Gent
BELGIUM
Liège
Maastricht
Köln
Kassel
Erfurt
Riesa
Dresden
Legnica
Wrocł
Brussels
(Bruxelles)
Siegen
Eisenach
Wałbrzych
Calais
Lens
Mons
Charleroi
Bonn
Koblenz
Suhl
Chemnitz
Opole
Dunkerque
Lille
Namur
LUX.
Wiesbaden
Zwickau
Coburg
Mladá
Boleslav
Liberec
Abbeville
Dieppe
Amiens
Saint-Quentin
Laon
Trier
Mainz
Frankfurt
Offenbach
Würzburg
Cheb
Kladno
Hradec Králové
Cap de la Hague
Cherbourg
Le Havre
Rouen
Mézières
Oise
Koblenz
Mannheim
Heidelberg
Heilbronn
Plzeň
PRAGUE
(PRAHA)
CZECH REPUBLIC
Ostrava
Pointe de Saint-Mathieu
GUERNSEY (U.K.)
CHANNEL IS.
JERSEY (U.K.)
Golfe de Saint Malo
Caen
Évreux
Reims
Châlons-sur-Marne
Metz
Saarbrücken
Karlsruhe
Nürnberg
Olomouc
Brest
Quimper
Saint-Brieuc
Saint-Malo
FRANCE
PARIS
Seine
Marne
Saint-Dizier
Heilbronn
Pointe du Raz
Lorient
Vannes
Rennes
Laval
Le Mans
Chartres
Alençon
Seine
DM-559100-2A-QR1- -1-1-1

ATLANTIC OCEAN

FAEROE ISLANDS (Den.)
Tórshavn

ROCKALL (U.K.)

SHETLAND ISLANDS
Lerwick
Sumburgh Head

RONA

SAINT KILDA

ORKNEY ISLANDS
Kirkwall
Wick
Duncansby Head

Cape Wrath
Stornoway
HEBRIDES
The Minch
Tobermory
Inverness
Moray Firth
Kinnaird Head
Ben Nevis 4,406
GRAMPIAN MTS.
SCOTLAND
Aberdeen
Dundee
Stirling
Perth
Glasgow
Edinburgh
UNITED
GREAT
Ayr
Kilmarnock
CHEVIOT HILLS
Newcastle upon Tyne
Sunderland
BRITISH ISLES
Bloody Foreland
Londonderry
Malin Head
North Channel
NORTHERN IRELAND
Ballymena
Belfast
Dumfries
Stranraer
Carlisle
Whitehaven
ENGLAND
Middlesbrough
Scarborough
KINGDOM
Erris Head
Achill Head
Donegal Bay
Sligo
Bangor
Dundalk
ISLE OF MAN (U.K.)
Douglas
York
Clifden
IRELAND
Galway
Irish Sea
Liverpool
Manchester
Chester
Bradford
Sheffield
Grimsby
Kingston upon Hull
Kilkee
Carrauntoohil 3,406
Limerick
Tipperary
Carlow
Dublin
Stoke on Trent
Derby
Nottingham
Leicester
Norwich
BRITAIN
Loop Head
Cork
Clonmel
Waterford
Shrewsbury
BIRMINGHAM
Coventry
Northampton
Cambridge
Great Yarmouth
Mizen Head
Kinsale
Bantry Bay
Dungarvan
St. George's Channel
Hereford
WALES
Newport
Oxford
Ipswich
Milford Haven
Swansea
Cardiff
Bristol
Reading
LONDON
Dover
CELTIC SEA
ISLES OF SCILLY
Land's End
Exeter
Southampton
Bournemouth
Brighton
Portsmouth
Strait of Dover
Penzance
Lizard Point
Plymouth
Start Point
English Channel

NORTH SEA

BALTI

Copyright by Rand McNally & Co.
Made in U.S.A.

Scale 1:10,000,000; one inch to 158 miles
Lambert Conformal Conic Projection

Copyright by Rand McNally & Co.
Made in U.S.A.
DM-559200-2A-QR1- -1-1-1

Scale 1:20,000,000; one inch to 315 miles
Lambert Azimuthal, Equal Area Projection

SEA
OF
OKHOTSK

OSTROV
SIMUSHIR

KURIL ISLANDS

SAKHALIN

OSTROV
URUP

OSTROV
ITURUP

The southern Kuril Islands
are occupied by Russia
pending a final peace
treaty.

OSTROV
KUNASHIR

La Perouse Strait

Wakkanai

Rumoi

Asahikawa

Mombetsu

Nayoro

Nemuro

SAPPORO

Kushiro

Otaru

HOKKAIDŌ

Muroran

Erimo-misaki

Hakodate

Tsugaru Kaikyo

Aomori

Hachinohe

Hirosaki

Morioka

Akita

Kamaishi

Ishinomaki

Sakata

Sendai

Yamagata

Fukushima

Niigata

Koriyama

Nagaoka

Iwaki

Hitachi

Nagano

Utsunomiya

Toyama

Maebashi

TŌKYŌ

Kanazawa

Matsumoto

KAWASAKI

Fukui

YOKOHAMA

Mt. Fuji
12,388

NAGOYA

Hamamatsu **JAPAN**

KYOTO

Nara

Tottori

KOBE

Yonago

OSAKA

Wakayama

Yonago

HIROSHIMA

Takamatsu

Kure

Matsuyama

Kochi

Shimonoseki

SHIKOKU

KITAKYŪSHU

Oita

FUKUOKA

Kumamoto

Sasebo

Miyazaki

Nagasaki

Miyakonojō

KYŪSHŪ

Kagoshima

Nishinoomote

TANEGA-SHIMA

YAKU-SHIMA

EAST
CHINA
SEA

RYUKYU ISLANDS (Japan)

Naze

AMAM-O-SHIMA

TOKUNO-SHIMA

PACIFIC OCEAN

Nago

OKINAWA-JIMA

Naha

Tropic of Cancer

Hirara

MIYAKO-JIMA

IRIOMOTE-
JIMA

ISHIGAKI-SHIMA

OKINO-TORI-SHIMA
(Japan)

SEA OF
JAPAN

RUSSIA

Chita

Sosnovo-
Ozerskoye

Aginskoye

Shilka

Sretensk

Mohe

Gulian

Amur

Svobodnyy

Komsomol'sk
na-Amure

Vysokogornyy

Porofaysk

Yuzhno-Sakhalinsk

Korsakov

Nevel'sk

Krasnogorsk

Udogorsk

Chaybalsan

Borzya

Zabaykal'sk

Manzhouli

Hailar

Qiqian

Hūma

Belogorsk

Blagoveshchensk

Raychikhinsk

Obluch'ye

Birobidzhan

Khabarovsk

Svetlaya

Krasnogorsk

Önderhaan

Baruun-Urt

Tamsagbulag

Butha Qi

Yitulihe

Nenjiang

Bei'an

HEILONGJIANG

Yichun

Suihua

Hegang

Jiamusi

Hulun
Nur

QIQIHAR

Anda

Hulan

HARBIN

Jixi

Lishegorsk

Ol'ga

Vladivostok

Nakhodka

Horqin Youyi Qianqi

Baicheng

Tongyu

Songhua

Mudanjiang

Pogranichnyy

Ussuriysk

Dalnerechensk

Bikin

Erenhot

Abag Qi

Bairin Zuoqi

Tongliao

Kailu

Shuangliao

CHANGCHUN

Jiutai

JILIN

Wangqing

Hunchun

Ch'ōngjin

Duanhua

Yanji

Najin

Öndörhaan

Abagner Qi

Linxi

Huide

Liaoyuan

JILIN

Huadian

Kanban

Kimch'aek

Duolun

Chifeng

Faku

Tonghua

Hyesan

Musan

Kilchu

Tanch'on

Taibus Qi

Weichang

SHENYANG

Benxi

Kanggye

Tanch'ōn

Ayan Obo

Jining

Beipiao

Chaoyang

Liaoyang

Pukchong

Manpo

FUSHUN

LIAONING

ANSHAN

Sakchu

Hamhūng

Hūngnam

Hohhot

Datong

Zhangjiakou

Xuanhua

Jinzhou

Dandong

Sinūiju

Anju

Wōnsan

NEI MONGGOL

Duolun

Yingkou

Qinhuangdao

Fuxian

Sunch'on

Sariwon

Sokch'o

Jungar Qi

Fengzhen

Miyun

GREAT WALL

Suizhong

P'YŎNGYANG

Namp'o

NORTH KOREA

Kaesong

Haeju

Kangnūng

BEIJING

Hangu

TANGSHAN

Lūshun

DALIAN

Korea
Bay

INCH'ŎN

Kaesŏng

SEOUL
(SŎUL)

Suweon

Wonju

Shiguaigou

Datong

TIANJIN

Bo Hai

Penglai

Weihai

Ch'ongju

Andong

SOUTH KOREA

OKI-SHOTŌ

Junggar Qi

TAIYUAN

SHIJIAZHUANG

Cangzhou

Huimin

Yantai

Laiyang

TAEJON

TAEGU

P'ohang

Yuci

Yangquan

HEBEI

Dezhou

Zibo

Shidao

Kunsan

Ulsan

Pingyao

SHANDONG

Yidu

Chŏnju

Masan

PUSAN

Xingtai

Handan

JINAN

Tai'an

Weifang

Chinju

Yosu

Korea
Strait

SHANXI

Changzhi

Anyang

Boshan

Xinwen

QINGDAO

KWANGJU

Yŏsu

Linfen

Jiaozuo

Xinxiang

Jining

Yishui

Linyi

Mokp'o

Yulin

Luoyang

Kaifeng

Heze

Tengxian

Rizhao

Lianyungang

Cheju

CHEJU DO
(S. Korea)

Sanmenxia

ZHENGZHOU

Xuchang

Shangqiu

JIANGSU

Yancheng

Pingdingshan

Luohe

Qingjiang

Baoying

Taizhou

Binhai

HENAN

Nanyang

Fuyang

Bengbu

Yangzhou

Zhenjiang

Nantong

Zhumadian

ANHUI

HUAINAN

Hefei

Changzhou

Wuxi

NANJING

Suzhou

Huangchuan

Xinyang

HUBEI

Suxian

Lu'an

Macheng

Wuhu

Huzhou

Jiaxing

SHANGHAI

Hangu

Zhongxiang

Anqing

Yangtze

HANGZHOU

Dinghai

Zhushan

Tianmen

WUHAN

Shashi

Huangshi

Jiujiang

Tunxi

Shaoxing

Ningbo

Yichang

Dayong

ZHEJIANG

Lanxi

Jinhua

Linhai

Changde

Jingdezhen

HUNAN

Yiyang

Nanchang

Shangrao

Quzhou

Lishui

Wenzhou

Yueyang

Xiangyin

CHANGSHA

Xinhua

Xiangtan

Zhuzhou

JIANGXI

Fuzhou

Rui'an

Shaoyang

Pingxiang

Nanchang

Wugang

Lingling

Hengyang

Ji'an

Nanping

Min

Luoyuan

Fuzhou

Chenxian

Xizhou

FUJIAN

Sanming

Minqing

Hirara

Shaoguan

Lianxian

Dayu

Ningdu

Changting

Putian

Chilung

Xinjiang

Qujiang

Huizhou

Ruijin

Quanzhou

T'AIPEI

Wangan

GUANGDONG

Chao'an

Xiamen

Zhangzhou

Hsinchu

Hira

Meixian

Changhua

Taichung

Hualien

Chiai

TAIWAN

Yu Shan
13,114

Guilin

Lianxian

Dayong

Shantou

T'ainan

Hezhou

GUANGZHOU

Foshan

Lufeng

Jiangmen

Kaiping

NEW KOWLOON

VICTORIA

Pingtung

KAOHSIUNG

T'AIWAN

Oluan Pi

Maoming

MACAO
(Port.)

HONG KONG
(U.K.)

Luzon Strait

**PHILIPPINE
SEA**

Zhanjiang

INDAO

Xuwen

TUNGSHA TAO
(Claimed by China, Taiwan)

BABUYAN
ISLANDS

Haikou

Wenchang

SOUTH CHINA SEA

Laoag

Aparri

PHILIPPINES

HAINAN

Taiwan Strait

Yellow
Sea

MANCHURIA

GREATER KHINGAN RANGE

WALL OF GENGHIS KHAN

GREAT WALL

Scale 1:16,000,000; one inch to 252 miles
Lambert Conformal Conic Projection

0   100   200   300   400   500 Miles

0   200   400   600   800 Kilometers

Tropic of Cancer

OKINO-TORI-SHIMA
(Japan)

MAUG ISLANDS

**PHILIPPINE
SEA**

**NORTHERN MARIANA
ISLANDS
(U.S.)**

MARIANA
ISLANDS

SARAGON

SAIPAN

Naga
Legaspi

PHILIPPINES

SAMAR

PACIFIC   OCEAN

GUAM
(U.S.)   Agana

Tacloban
LEYTE
Bacolod
Cebu

Tagbilaran

Dumaguete

SOROL

YAP

Sibuyan Sea

Cagayan de Oro

Maravi   Bislig

MINDANAO

Mount
Apo
9,692

Davao

Cotabato

FEDERATED STATES OF
MICRONESIA

GAFEKUT

Koronadal

General Santos

Cape San Agustin

PALAU ISLANDS   Koror

Tinaca
Point

KEPULAUAN
TALAUD

SONSORAL
ISLANDS

Tahuna

PALAU (BELAU)

CAROLINE ISLANDS

MOROTAI
Galela   Wayabula

Manado   Gunung Klabat 6,634
Tondano

HALMAHERA

Weda

Equator

Molucca Sea
(Laut Maluku)

M
O
L
U
C
C
A
S

Labuha

Laiwui

KEPULAUAN OBI

KEPULAUAN SULU

Tanjung Liboba

Sorong

Jazirah Doberai

Manokwari

MANUS
ISLAND   Patusi

Bosnik

Teba   Tanjung D'Urville
Sarmi

BISMARCK ARCHIPELAGO

Kavieng

Serui

Ceram Sea
(Laut Seram)

PULAU MISOOL

Kokas

Teluk
Cenderawasih

Waren

Jayapura

Wewak

Piru

Namlea
BURU

CERAM (SERAM)

Bula

Semenanjung
Bomberai

Mamberamo

Sepik

Bogia

Ambon

PEGUNUNGAN MAOKE

NEW   GUINEA

CENTRAL RANGE

Madang

E
S
I
A

(
M
A
L
U
K
U
)

Tual

Dobo

Puncak
Jaya
16,503

Puncak
Trikora
15,584

Puncak
Mandala
15,617

Mount Hagen

Mount
Wilhelm
14,793

Goroka

Aiseqa

Hoskins

Banda Sea
(Laut Banda)

Birab

Kepi

KEPULAUAN
ARU

Tanjung De Jongs

Lake
Murray

Mount
Giluwe
14,330

Karema

Lae

Cape Cretin

AWU

NEW BRITAIN

KEPULAUAN BARAT DAYA

PULAU YAMDENA

Tepa

Saumlaki

PULAU YOS
SUDARSO

Tanjung Vals

Digul

Fly

Meraukе

**PAPUA NEW
GUINEA**

Popondetta

Tufi

Losuia

Dili

TIMOR

Tutuala

Soe

Ocussi

Timor Sea

ARAFURA SEA

Daru

Mari

Gulf of
Papua

OWEN STANLEY RANGE

Esa ala

Samarai

Port Moresby

Torres Strait

Bamaga   Cape York

0   100   200   300   400   500 Miles

0   200   400   600   800 Kilometers

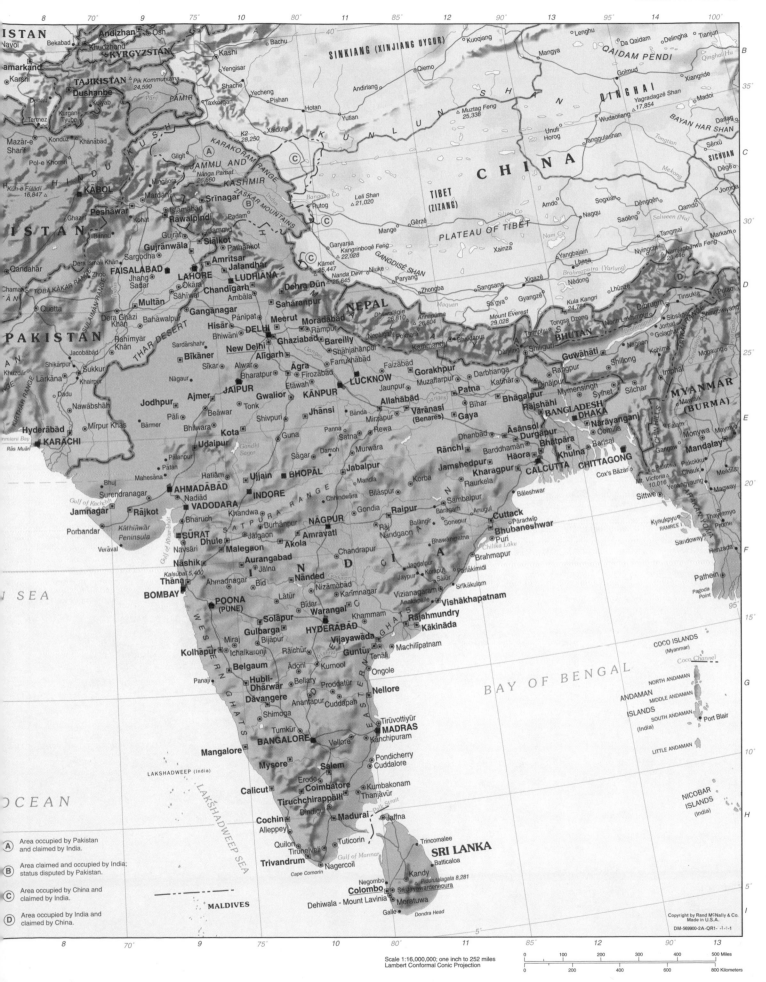

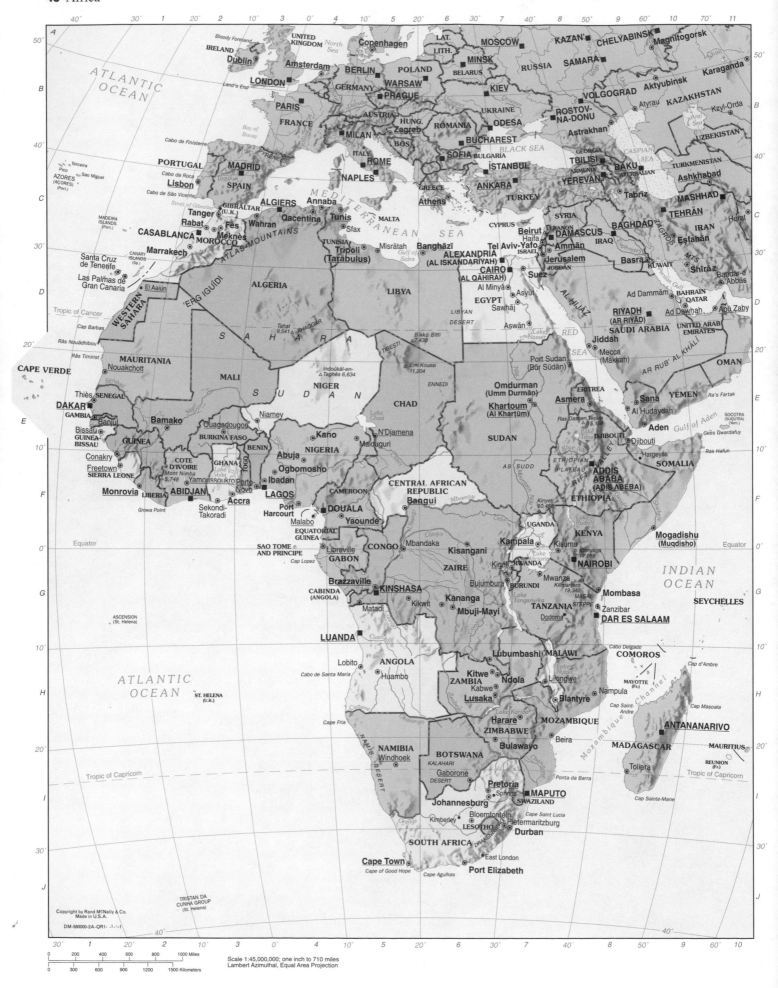

Scale 1:45,000,000; one inch to 710 miles
Lambert Azimuthal, Equal Area Projection

NIG.
Bamenda
Foumban
Meiganga
Bouar
Bertoua
Oya
CENTRAL AFRICAN REPUBLIC
Bossembélé
Bambari
Zémio
Obo
Tambura
SUDAN
Bor
Gugo 13,780
Mali
Dima
Kibre Menglst
A
Calabar
Nkongsamba
CAMEROON
Yakoma
Bondo
Yambio
Yei
Juba
Kheyti 10,456
Tonj
Lokichokio
North Horr
Mega
RIFT VALLEY
ETHIOPIA
Kumba
DOUALA
Edéa
Mbalmayo
Yaoundé
Nola
Mbaiki
Berbérati
Yakoma
Bondo
Niangara
Isiro
Watsa
Faradje
Arua
Gulu
Kitale
Mount Elgon 14,178
Eldoret
Marsabit
North Horr
South Horr
Doolow
Malabo
BIOKO
(EQUAT. GU.)
Kribi
Ebolowa
Ouesso
Gemena
Lisala
Bumba
Basoko
Bafwasende
Beni
Butembo
Fort Portal
Mbale
Soroti
Kampala
Entebbe
Jinja
Mado Gashi
Wajir
Baardheere
Domadare
B
Bata
EQUAT. GUINEA
Oyem
Mitzic
Mékambo
Makokou
CONGO
Mbandaka
Boende
Bokungu
Opala
Lubutu
Margherita Peak 16,763
Kisangani
Mbarara
Masaka
UGANDA
Kisumu
Kericho
Nakuru
KENYA
Nyeri
Kirinyaga 17,058
Garissa
Afmadow
Jamaame
Kismaayo
SOMALIA
Libreville
GABON
Lambaréné
Lastoursville
Ewo
Gamboma
Bikoro
Iketa
Equator
Lac
Mai-Ndombe
Walikale
Volcan Karisimbi 14,187
Rwanda
Kigali
Lake Victoria
Musoma
UKEREWE ISLAND
Kahama
NAIROBI
Machakos
0°
Cap Lopez
Port Gentil
Koulamoutou
Franceville
Zanaga
Djambala
Bandundu
Ilebo
Bukavu
Kalima
Biharamulo
Mwanza
Lamu
Settê Cama
Tchibanga
Ndendé
ZAIRE
Kindu
Lodja
Mweka
Lusambo
Kasongo
Bujumbura
BURUNDI
Tabora
Malindi
Mombasa
C
Mayumba
Pointe-Noire
Dolisie
Brazzaville
KINSHASA
Kikwit
Kananga
Mbuji-Mayi
Mwene-Ditu
Kaniama
Mpanda
Uvinza
Kalemie
MASAI STEPPE
Tanga
PEMBA
CABINDA (Angola)
Boma
Matadi
Mbanza-Ngungu
Tshikapa
Ugoma 9,780
Kabalo
Kongolo
Kahama
TANZANIA
Dodoma
Morogoro
Zanzibar
5°
LUANDA
Ambriz
Camabatela
Marimpa
Caúngula
Kamina
Bukama
Lake Tanganyika
Lake Rukwa
Sumbawanga
Mbala
Iringa
DAR ES SALAAM
D
Nóqui
Damba
Chiluage
Kasaji
KATANGA
Dilolo
Kolwezi
Likasi
Kasama
Mbeya
Karonga
Manda
Nachingwea
Lindi
Mtwara
Cabo Delgado
Palma
Serra do Môco 8,596
Kuito
ANGOLA
Cassai
Mwinilunga
Lubumbashi
Chingola
Mufulira
Kitwe
Lundazi
Lake Nyasa
Lichinga
Maua
Ibo
Quissanga
Pemba
Lúrio
Nacala
E
Lobito
Benguela
Lucira
Huambo
Malanje
Sáurimo
Cangumbe
MONTS MITUMBA
Kasempa
Luanshya
Ndola
Kabwe
Mandimba
Nampula
Moçambique
Mogincual
Moma
Cabo de Santa Maria
Lubango
Cassinga
Cuito-Cuanavale
Mavinga
N'Riquinha
ZAMBIA
Lusaka
Mazabuka
Choma
Tete
Sapitwa 9,849
Blantyre
RIFT VALLEY
Quelimane
F
Namibe
Ponta da Marca
Chitado
Cuangar
Shakawe
CAPRIVI STRIP
Livingstone
Kadoma
Lake Kariba
Kariba
Nyangani 8,504
Monte Binga 7,992
Beira
Nova Sofala
INDIAN OCEAN
Cape Fria
Sesfontein
Namutoni
Grootfontein
Maun
Hwange
Gwai
Bulawayo
ZIMBABWE
Harare
Mutare
Chimoio
MOZAMBIQUE
Nova Mambone
20°
Palgrave Point
Brandberg 8,461
Kaap Kruis
Outjo
Otavi
Toteng
Gwanda
West Nicholson
Gweru
Masvingo
Espungabera
Ponta São Sebastião
G
NAMIB DESERT
NAMIBIA
Swakopmund
Walvis Bay
Gobabis
Windhoek
Tshwaane
BOTSWANA
Serowe
Palapye
Francistown
Selebi Phikwe
Tuli
Messina
Louis Trichardt
Massangena
Massinga
Inhambane
Ponta da Barra
j
KALAHARI DESERT
Tshane
Shoshong
Mariental
Gibeon
Khakhea
Gaborone
Kanye
Pietersburg
Potgietersrus
TRANSVAAL
Nelspruit
Xai-Xai
Inharrime
k
Tropic of Capricorn
Lüderitz
Keetmanshoop
Seeheim
Tshabong
Pretoria
Springs
Mbabane
MAPUTO
Cabo de Santa Maria
H
Aus
Aroab
Hotazel
Johannesburg
Klerksdorp
Vereeniging
SWAZILAND
Lomba
Oranjemund
Alexander Bay
Karasburg
Warmbad
Upington
Kimberley
Vryburg
Welkom
Kroonstad
Vrede
Dundee
Cape Saint Lucia
Port Nolloth
BUSHMAN LAND
Bloemfontein
Maseru
eNjesuthi 11,306
Thabana-Ntlenyana 11,425
LESOTHO
Pietermaritzburg
Durban
30°
SOUTH AFRICA
Brandvlei
Vanrhynsdorp
Middelburg
Queenstown
Umtata
Port Shepstone
Port Edward
ATLANTIC OCEAN
Lambert's Bay
Clanwilliam
Beaufort West
GREAT KARROO
Graaff-Reinet
Uitenhage
Grahamstown
East London
I
Cape Columbine
Piketberg
Pearl
Worcester
Oudtshoorn
Humansdorp
Port Elizabeth
Cape Town
Cape of Good Hope
Bredasdorp
Cape Agulhas
35°

Cap d'Ambre
Antsiranana
Hell-Ville
Ambanja
j
Mahajanga
Maromokotro 9,436
Analalava
Marovoay
Cap Saint-André
Tamborano
Cap Masoala
k
Morafenobe
Ambatondrazaka
Lac Alaotra
Toamasina
Maintirano
ANTANANARIVO
Antsirabe
Mahanoro
MADAGASCAR
Morondava
Ambositra
Mananjary
l
Fianarantsoa
Ihosy
Pic Boby 8,720
Manakara
m
Toliara
Androka
Tropic of Capricorn
INDIAN OCEAN
Cap Sainte-Marie
Ambovombe
Faradofay
n

Scale 1:20,000,000; one inch to 315 miles
Sinusoidal Projection

0 100 200 300 400 500 600 Miles
0 200 400 600 800 1000 Kilometers

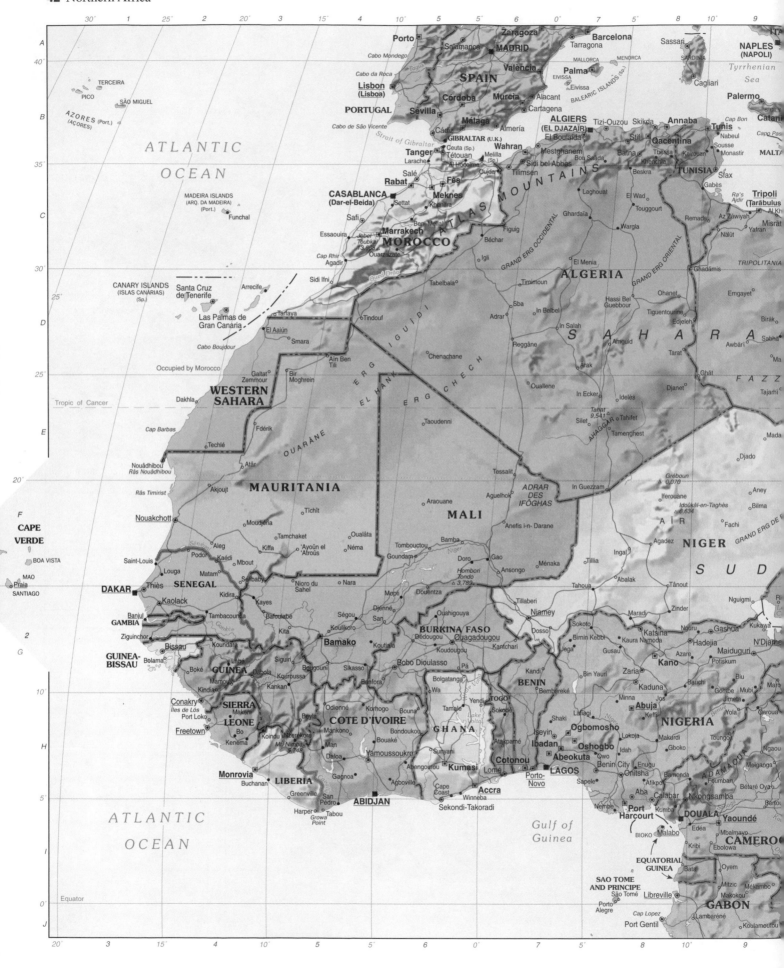

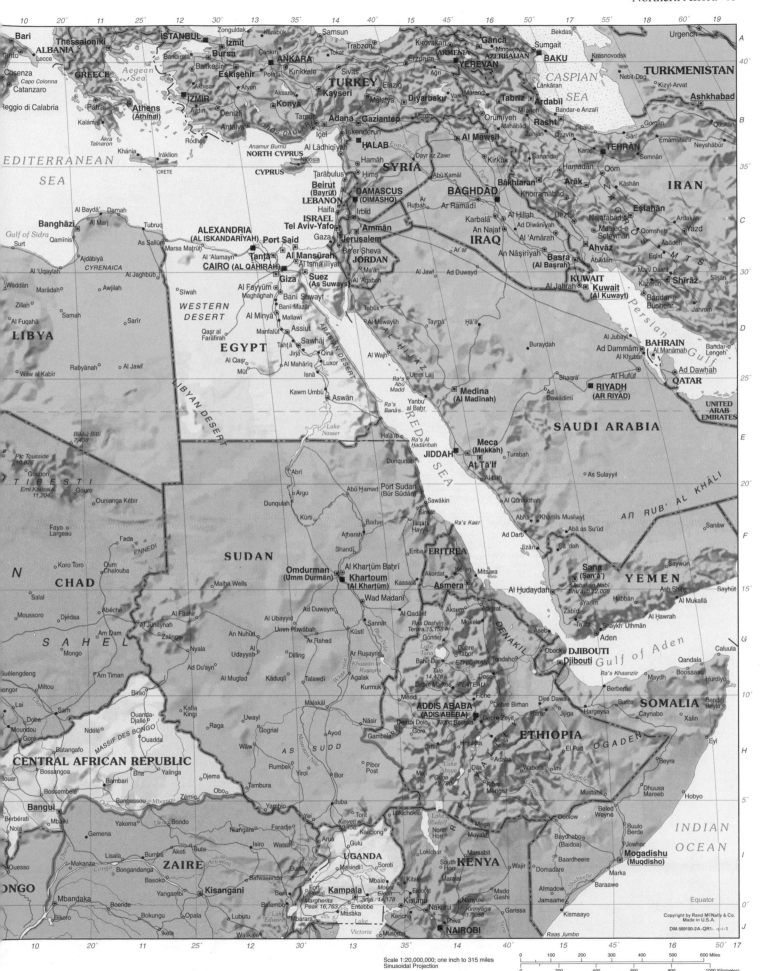

Bari
Thessaloniki
ALBANIA
Lecce
Cosenza
Capo Colonna
Catanzaro
Reggio di Calabria
GREECE
Aegean
Sea
Kalámai
Átmos
Tainaron
Pátrai
Athens
(Athínai)
Khániá
CRETE
Iráklion
Rhódos

ISTANBUL
Bursa
Bandirma
Balikesir
Eskişehir
IZMIR
Aydin
Denizli
Antalya

Zonguldak
Karabük
Ankara
Çankiri
Polatlı
Konya
Tarsus
İçel
Anamur Burnu
NORTH CYPRUS
Nicosia
CYPRUS

Samsun
Kayseri
Sivas
Tokat
Yozgat
Kirikkale
Afyon
Aksaray

TURKEY
Kırşehir
Elaziğ
Malatya
Gaziantep
Iskenderun
Halab
Hamáh
Tarábulus
Himş

Trabzon
Erzurum
Ağrı
Diyarbakır
Van
Mardin
Dayr az Zawr
Abū Kamāl

Kirovakan
ARMENIA
Yerevan
Azerbaijan
Erzurum
Marand
Ōrūmiyeh
Mahābād
Zahjān
Sanandaj
Kirkūk

Bekdaş
Gäncä
Mingäçevir
Baku
Sumgait

Urgench
Krasnovodsk
TURKMENISTAN
Nebit-Dag
Kizyl-Arvat

CASPIAN
SEA

Ashkhabad

Tabriz
Ardabil
Bandar-e Anzali
Rasht
Qazvin
Tehrān

Mianeh
Zanjān
Hamadān
Qom
Karaj

Gorgan
Quchan
Neyshābūr
Sari
Emämshahr
Semnan

IRAN

MEDITERRANEAN
SEA

Al Baydā'
Darnah
Banghāzī
Al Marj
Gulf of Sidra
Surt
Qaminis

Tubruq
As Sallūm
Marsa Matrūh

Alexandria
(Al Iskandarīyah)
Port Said
Al 'Alamayn
Tanta
Cairo (Al Qāhirah)
Giza
Al Fayyūm
Maghāghah
Banī Suwayf
Banī Mazār
Al Minyā
Mallawī
Manfalūt
Assiut
Sawhāj
Tahtā
Jirja
Qinā
Luxor
Al Mahārīq
Isnā
Kawm Umbū
Aswān

Port Said
Al Manşūrah
Al Ismā'īlīyah
Suez
(As Suways)

Beirut
(Bayrūt)
LEBANON
Haifa
ISRAEL
Tel Aviv-Yafo
'Ammān
Jerusalem
Be'er Sheva
Gaza
JORDAN
Ma'ān
Al 'Aqabah
Tabūk
Al Muwaylih

DAMASCUS
(DIMASHQ)
SYRIA
Irbid
Ar Rutbah
Ar Ramādī
Karbalā'
An Najaf
Ar'ar
Al Jawf
Ad Duwayd

BAGHDAD
Al Hillah
Ad Dīwānīyah
An Nāşirīyah
Al 'Amārah
Baṣrah
(Al Başrah)
IRAQ

HALAB
Dayr az Zawr
Al Mawşil

Bākhtiarī
Arāk
Khorramābād
Dezfūl
Najafābād
Masjed-e
Soleymān
Ahvāz
Ābādān
Eqlīd
Marv Dasht

Esfahān
Ardakān
Yazd
Abādeh
Qomsheh
Shīrāz
Sīrjān

MTS

Kuwait
Al Jahrah
Kuwait
(Al Kuwayt)

Kāzerūn
Bandar-e
Büshehr
Jahrom

Najd

WESTERN
DESERT

Al Jawf
Al 'Uqaylah
Waddan
Marādah
Awjilah
Zillah
Al Fuqahā'
Samah
Sarīr

Sīwah
Al Jaghbūb

Taymā'
Hā'il

Buraydah
Shaqrā'
Ad
Dawādīmī

Ad Dammām
Al Manāmah
Al Khubār
Al Hufūf

BAHRAIN
Bandar-e
Lengeh
Gulf
Ad Dawhah
QATAR

UNITED
ARAB
EMIRATES

LIBYA
Waw al Kabir
Rabyānah
Al Jawf

Qasr al
Farāfirah
Al Qaşr
Mūt
Dākhla

Al Wajh
Yanbu'
al Bahr
Ra's
Banās
Halā'ib
Ra's
Abū
Madd

Medina
(Al Madīnah)
RIYADH
(AR RIYĀD)

SAUDI ARABIA

Pic Toussidé
10,876
Bikkū Bitti
7,438
Goubon
TIBESTI
Emi Koussis
11,204
Gouro
Ounianga Kébir
Faya
Largeau
ENNEDI
Fada

Abrī
Argo
Dunqulah
Kürti
Berber

Lake
Nasser

Dunqunab
Port Sudan
(Būr Sūdān)
Sawākin
Sinkat
Tōkar

Meca
(Makkah)
At Tā'if
Al Līth
Al Qunfudhah
Abhā
Ad Darb
Jīzān
Sa'dah

Turabah
As Sulayyil
Abā as Su'ūd

RED
SEA

AN RUB' AL KHĀLĪ

Sanāw

CHAD
Koro Toro
Oum
Chalouba
Salal
Moussoro
Djédaa
Abéché
Am Dam
Mongo
Guélengdeng
Miltou
Bongor

Malha Wells
Al Fāshir
Al Junaynah
Nyala
An Nuhūd
Umm Ruwābah
Ad Du'ayn
Al Muglad
Am Timan

Atbarah
Shandi
Khartūm Bahrī
Omdurman
(Umm Durmān)
Khartoum
(Al Khartūm)
Wad Madanī
Kassalā
Al Qadārif
Sannār
Kūstī
Ar Rahad
Dilling
Kāduqlī
Talawdī

SUDAN

Barka
Eriba
Ra's Kasar

ERITREA
Keren
Mitsiwa
Akordat
Asmera

Khamīs Mushayt
Jizān

Aksum
Adigrat
Ras Dashen
Terara 15,158
Gonder
Mekele
DENAKIL

Sa'dah
Jabal an Nabī
Shu'ayb 12,008
Sana
(San'ā')
Yarīm
Zabīd
Ta'izz
Al Hudaydah
Habbān
Ash Shihr
Al Mukallā
Shaykh 'Uthmān
Aden

Saywūn
Sayhūt

YEMEN

Gulf of Aden

SAHEL

CENTRAL AFRICAN REPUBLIC
Bossangoa
Batangafo
Bossembélé
Bangui
Berbérati
Nola
Mbaïki

Birao
Ndélé
Ouanda-
Djallé
Ouadda
MASSIF DES BONGO
Bria
Yalinga
Bambari
Bangassou
Zémio
Obo
Yakoma
Bondo

Kafia
Kingi
Raga
Uwayl
Gogrial
Wāw
AS SUDD
Rumbek
Yirol
Djema
Tambura
Yambio
Yei
Faradje
Niangara
Watsa
Isiro

Malakāl
Nāşir
Ayod
Pibor
Post
Bor
Torit
Juba
Gulu
Aru
Arua

Dembī Dolo
Gambela
Gore
Jīma
Agalak
Kurmuk
Mandi
Akobo
Bale

Bahir Dar
Lake
Tana
Debre
Tabor
Tālo
14,478
Debre Markos
ETHIOPIAN
PLATEAU
Fiche
ADDIS ABABA
(ADIS ABEBA)
Akaki Beseka
Hosaina
Asela
Gugé
13,780
Dīla
Mega
Moyale
Soddo
Yavello

Debre Birhan
Debre Zeyit
Nazrēt
Harer
Dire Dawa
Jijiga
Hargeysa
El Fud
Imī
Wabera
Sela
Mustahīl

DJIBOUTI
Djibouti
Obock
Tendaho
Asela
Āsela

OGADEN

SOMALIA
Burco
Caynabo
Xalin
Beyra
Eyl

Qandala
Boosaaso
Maydh
Berbera
Ras Khaanziir
Caluula

Bender
Beyla
Hurdiyo

ZAIRE
Kisangani
Bumba
Aketi
Buta
Basoko
Yangambi
Boende
Opala
Ikela
Walikale
Lubutu
Butembo
Beni

UGANDA
Kampala
Fort
Portal
Masindi
Soroti
Mbale
Entebbe
Masaka
Mbarara
Margherita
Peak 16,763
Lake
Edward

Lake
Victoria

Gulu
Lira
Kitgum
Lokichar
Lodwar
North
Horr
South
Horr
Lokichokio
Marsabit
Kaabong
Mount
Elgon
14,178
Eldoret
Kisumu
Nakuru
Kericho
Musoma

NAIROBI
Thika
Nyeri
Nanyuki
Kirinyaga
17,058
Garissa
Wajir

KENYA
Baardheere
Domadare
Doolow
Buulo
Berde
Baydhabo
(Baidoa)
Jowhar
Mogadishu
(Muqdisho)
Marka
Baraawe
Kismaayo
Raas Jumbo
Jamaame
Afmadow
Buur Gaabo

INDIAN
OCEAN

Equator

Copyright by Rand McNally & Co.
Made in U.S.A.

DM-589100-2A-QR1

Scale 1:20,000,000; one inch to 315 miles
Sinusoidal Projection

0   100   200   300   400   500   600 Miles
0   200   400   600   800   1000 Kilometers

RUSSIA

SEA OF OKHOTSK

BERING SEA

SAKHALIN

Poluostrov Kamchatka

ALEUTIAN ISLAND

International Date Line

KURIL ISLANDS

HOKKAIDO

SEA OF JAPAN

Vladivostok

SAPPORO

HIMALAYAS

Kathmandu

NEPAL

BHU.

INDIA

BNGL

CHINA

XI'AN

Mekong

BEIJING

SHENYANG

NORTH KOREA

P'YŎNGYANG

SEOUL

SOUTH KOREA

TIANJIN

QINGDAO

PUSAN

KITAKYŪSHŪ

KŌBE

JAPAN

HONSHŪ

Fuji san 12,388

TŌKYŌ

YOKOHAMA

Chongqing

WUHAN

NANJING

SHANGHAI

Yangtze

KYŪSHŪ

PACIFIC

CHITTAGONG

MYANMAR (BURMA)

GUANGZHOU

Ha Noi

MACAO (Port.)

HONG KONG (U.K.)

T'AIPEI

TAIWAN

KAOHSIUNG

Tropic of Cancer

LAOS

Hai Phong

HAINAN DAO

YANGON

Viangchan

THAILAND

SOUTH CHINA SEA

Escarpada Point

LUZON

PHILIPPINE SEA

MICRONESIA

NORTHERN MARIANA ISLANDS (U.S.)

MARIANA ISLANDS

VIETNAM

Da Nang

BANGKOK

CAMBODIA

MANILA

QUEZON CITY

PHILIPPINES

GUAM (U.S.)

MARSHALL ISLANDS

Phnum Pénh

THANH PHO HO CHI MINH (SAIGON)

Mui Ca Mau

Cebu

Zamboanga

MINDANAO

Davao

Gunong Kinabalu 13,455

Koror

PALAU ISLANDS

FEDERATED STATES OF MICRONESIA

MALAYSIA

Bandar Seri Begawan

BRUNEI

PALAU (BELAU)

CAROLINE ISLANDS

KIRIBATI

KIRI

Kuala Lumpur

SINGAPORE

BORNEO (KALIMANTAN)

Equator

NAURU

PHOENIX ISLA

Gunung Kerinci 12,467

SUMATRA

PALEMBANG

Banjarmasin

CELEBES

CERAM

INDONESIA

NEW GUINEA

Puncak Jaya 16,503

NEW BRITAIN

BOUGAINVILLE

SOLOMON ISLANDS

MELANESIA

TUVALU

TOKE

JAKARTA

SURABAYA

JAVA

Mt. Giluwe 14,330

PAPUA NEW GUINEA

Port Moresby

Honiara

SANTA CRUZ ISLANDS

WALLIS AND FUTUNA (Fr.)

SA

WESTERN SAMOA

Tanjung Vals

Cape York

ARAFURA SEA

TIMOR

TIMOR SEA

CHRISTMAS ISLAND (Austl.)

CORAL SEA

VANUATU

Port Vila

NEW CALEDONIA (Fr.)

FIJI

VANUA LEVU

VITI LEVU

Suva

TONG

Darwin

Cape Londonderry

Gulf of Carpentaria

York Peninsula

Cooktown

Cairns

NOUVELLE CALÉDONIE

Nouméa

Cape Leveque

Normanton

Townsville

GREAT DIVIDING RANGE

Cape Capricorn

Cape Capricorn

INDIAN OCEAN

North West Cape

GREAT SANDY DESERT

Alice Springs

Sandy Cape

NORFOLK ISLAND (Austl.)

AUSTRALIA

Ayers Rock 2,844

Brisbane

Carnarvon

Carnegie

Tropic of Capricorn

GREAT VICTORIA DESERT

Darling

Newcastle

Sydney

North Cape

Auckland

East Cape

NORTH ISLAND

Mt. Ruapehu 9,177

Wanneroo

Perth

Kalgoorlie-Boulder

Port Augusta

Adelaide

Great Australian Bight

Mt. Kosciusko 7,310

Canberra

TASMAN SEA

Cape Arid

Cape Naturaliste

Hood Point

Cape Carnot

Cape Jaffa

Melbourne

Cape Howe

Cape Farewell

Wellington

NEW ZEALAND

Christchurch

SOUTH ISLAND

Point D'Entrecasteaux

Cape Grim

TASMANIA

Cape Otway

Cape Portland

Mt. Ossa 5,305

Hobart

Mt. Cook 12,316

Cape Providence

CHATHAM ISLANDS

South East Cape

STEWART ISLAND

International Date Line

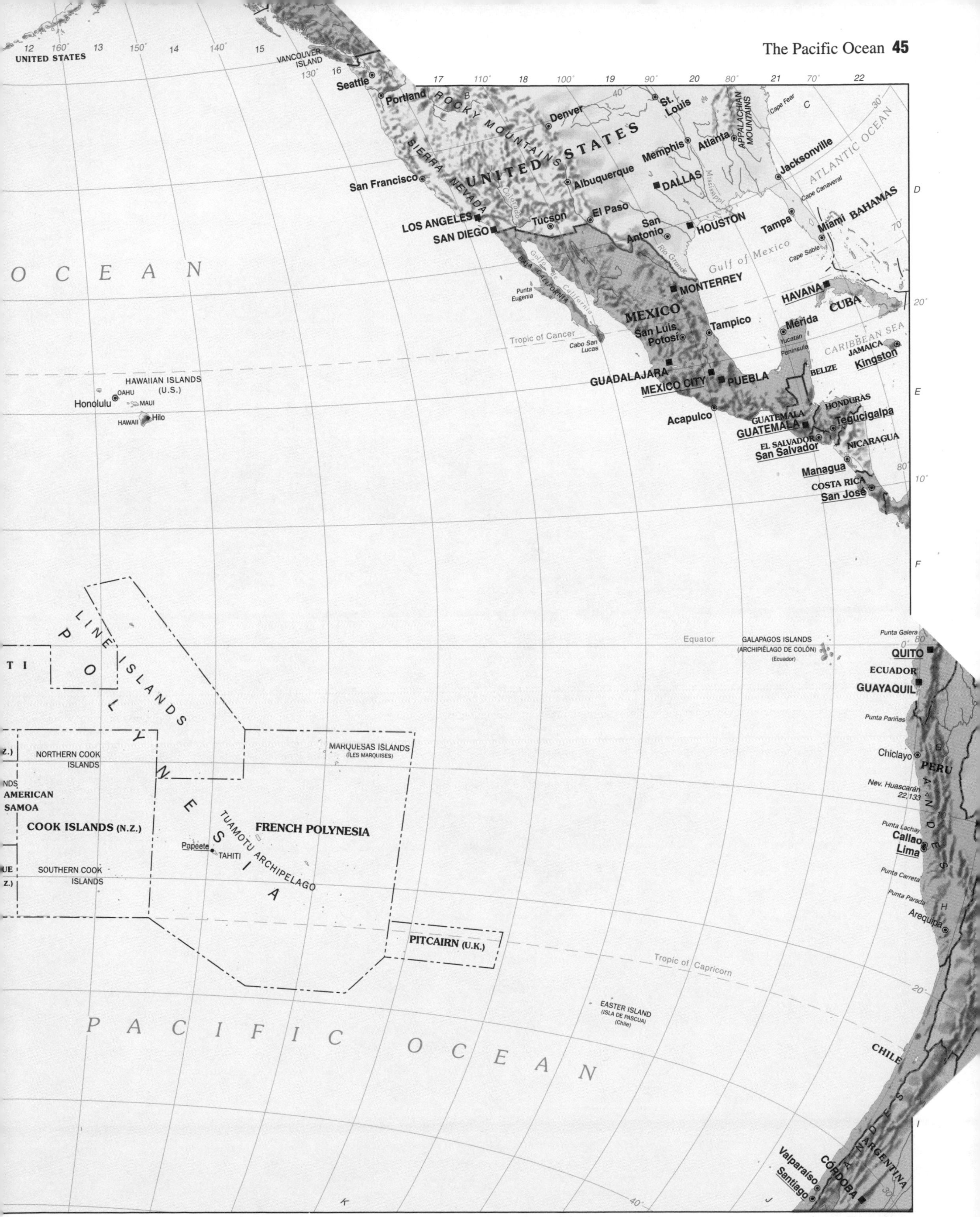

12 160° 13 150° 14 140° 15 130° 16 120° 17 110° 18 100° 19 90° 20 80° 21 70° 22

UNITED STATES

VANCOUVER ISLAND

Seattle
Portland

ROCKY MOUNTAIN

Denver
St. Louis

Cape Fear

ATLANTIC OCEAN

UNITED STATES

SIERRA NEVADA

San Francisco

Albuquerque
Memphis
Atlanta

APPALACHIAN MOUNTAINS

Jacksonville

Cape Canaveral

LOS ANGELES
SAN DIEGO

Tucson
El Paso

San Antonio
DALLAS

HOUSTON

Tampa

Miami BAHAMAS

Cape Sable

Punta Eugenia

Gulf of Mexico

BAJA CALIFORNIA

Gulf of California

MONTERREY

HAVANA

CUBA

MEXICO

Rio Grande

Tropic of Cancer

San Luis Potosí

Tampico

Mérida

CARIBBEAN SEA

Cabo San Lucas

Yucatan Peninsula

JAMAICA
Kingston

O C E A N

HAWAIIAN ISLANDS (U.S.)

GUADALAJARA
MEXICO CITY
PUEBLA

BELIZE

Honolulu

OAHU
MAUI

Acapulco

GUATEMALA
GUATEMALA

HONDURAS

Tegucigalpa

HAWAII
Hilo

EL SALVADOR
San Salvador

NICARAGUA

Managua

COSTA RICA
San José

LINE ISLANDS

POLYNESIA

Equator

GALAPAGOS ISLANDS
(ARCHIPIÉLAGO DE COLÓN)
(Ecuador)

Punta Galera

QUITO

ECUADOR

GUAYAQUIL

Punta Pariñas

NORTHERN COOK ISLANDS

MARQUESAS ISLANDS
(ÎLES MARQUISES)

Chiclayo

PERU

AMERICAN SAMOA

Nev. Huascarán 22,133

COOK ISLANDS (N.Z.)

TUAMOTU ARCHIPELAGO

FRENCH POLYNESIA

Punta Lachay
Callao
Lima

Papeete
TAHITI

SOUTHERN COOK ISLANDS

Punta Carreta

Punta Parada

Arequipa

PITCAIRN (U.K.)

Tropic of Capricorn

EASTER ISLAND
(ISLA DE PASCUA)
(Chile)

CHILE

P A C I F I C   O C E A N

ARGENTINA

Valparaíso
Santiago

CÓRDOBA

12 160° 13 150° 14 130° 15 130° 16 120° 17 110° 18 100° 19 90° 20 80° 21 70° 22 60°

Scale 1:45,000,000; one inch to 710 miles
Lambert Azimuthal, Equal Area Projection

0 200 400 600 800 1000 Miles
0 300 600 900 1200 1500 Kilometers

SOLOMON SEA

NEW BRITAIN
Cape Cretin
Lae
Popondetta
BOUGAINVILLE
Kulumadau
Port
Moresby
Samarai
OWEN STANLEY RANGE

CHOISEUL
SANTA ISABEL
SOLOMON
ISLANDS
Honiara
MALAITA
GUADALCANAL
SAN CRISTOBAL

TUVALU

CORAL SEA

Cairns
Bartle Frere
5,322
Halifax Bay
Townsville

SANTA CRUZ
ISLANDS

VANUATU
ÎLES BANKS
ESPIRITU SANTO
PENTECATE
MALAKULA
EPI
Port Vila
ÉFATÉ
NEW
ERROMANGO
HEBRIDES

WALLIS
AND
FUTUNA
(Fr.)

FIJI
VANUA
LEVU
Lautoka
VITI
LEVU
Suva
KANDUVU
ISLAND

Mackay
Mt. Dalrymple
4,131
Blair Athol
Rockhampton
Cape
Capricorn
Emerald
Gladstone
Springsure
caldine
Theodore
ackall
Bundaberg
Mitchell
Chinchilla
Sandy Cape
FRASER ISLAND
Maryborough
Gympie
Mt. Kiangarow
△ 3,760
Redcliffe
arieville
Toowoomba
Brisbane
Ipswich
Cunnamulla
DARLING
Warwick
Southport
DOWNS
Cape Byron
Lismore

NEW
CALEDONIA
(Fr.)
NOUVELLE
CALÉDONIE
LOYALTY
ISLANDS
Nouméa

PACIFIC

OCEAN

Tropic of Capricorn

Doube
Grafton
Nyngan
Coffs
Harbour
Tamworth
Armidale
Dubbo
Taree
H WALES
Cessnock
Newcastle
Griffith
Penrith
Parramatta
Sydney
Goulburn
Campbelltown
Wollongong
Wagga
Wagga
A.C.T.
Canberra
Jervis Bay
Albury
ngaratta
D
Cooma
Mt. Kosciusko
7,310
RIA
Cape Howe
lbourne
Sale
og
Wilsons Promontory

NORFOLK ISLAND
(Austl.)

TASMAN

nie Devonport
Cape Portland
han Launceston
Mt. Ossa
5,305
Freycinet Peninsula
TASMANIA
Hobart
South East Cape

FLINDERS ISLAND

SEA

North
Cape
Cape Maria
van Diemen
Cape Brett
Whangarei
Needles Point
Mount Roskill
East Coast Bays
Manukau
Auckland
Hamilton
Bay of Plenty
Albatross Point
Tauranga
NORTH ISLAND
Rotorua
New Plymouth
East Cape
Cape
Egmont
Taupo
Mt. Ruapehu
Wanganui
Gisborne
Napier
Cape Farewell
Palmerston North
Hastings
The Twins
5,980
Nelson
Porirua
Cook Strait
Greymouth
Wellington
SOUTH ISLAND
Whataroa
NEW
ZEALAND
Jackson Head
Haast
Mt.
SOUTHERN ALPS
Christchurch
West Cape
Ashburton
Manapouri
Timaru
Invercargill
Oamaru
Foveaux Strait
Dunedin
STEWART
ISLAND

CHATHAM
ISLANDS
(N.Z.)

International Date Line

Scale 1:20,000,000; one inch to 315 miles
Lambert's Azimuthal; Equal Area Projection

0   100   200   300   400   500   600 Miles
0   200   400   600   800   1000 Kilometers

PACIFIC OCEAN

ATLANTIC OCEAN

INDIAN OCEAN

Rosario

BUENOS AIRES

URUGUAY
MONTEVIDEO

BRAZIL

ARGENTINA

CHILE

ANDES

PATAGONIA

ARCHIPIÉLAGO
DE LOS
CHONOS

Strait of
Magellan

TIERRA
DEL FUEGO

Cape Horn

DRAKE PASSAGE

FALKLAND ISLANDS
(U.K.)

SOUTH SHETLAND
ISLANDS (U.K.)

Palmer
Station
(U.S.)

ADELAIDE I.

ALEXANDER I.

Bellingshausen
Sea

THURSTON I.

Amundsen
Sea

Mt. Siple
10,203

Mt. Sidley
13,717

Mt. Ulmer
8,996

Vinson Massif
16,066

ELLSWORTH
MTS.

Mt. Rex
3,625

LARSEN
ICE SHELF

SOUTH GEORGIA
(U.K.)

Scotia Sea

SOUTH ORKNEY
ISLANDS U.K.)

SOUTH SANDWICH
ISLANDS (U.K.)

RONNE
ICE SHELF

Weddell Sea

BERKNER I.

FILCHNER
ICE SHELF

COATS
LAND

Cape
Norvegia

MARIE
BYRD
LAND

ROCKEFELLER
PLATEAU

WHITMORE
MTS.

THIEL
MTS.

PENSACOLA
MTS.

QUEEN MAUD LAND

MÜHLIG
HOFMANN
MTS.

ROOSEVELT I.

QUEEN
MAUD
MTS.

Amundsen - Scott
South Pole Station
(U.S.)
South Pole

Ross
Sea

ROSS ICE
SHELF

Cape
Adare

McMurdo Station (U.S.)

Mt. Erebus
12,451

Mt. Minto 13,658

Mt. Markham
14,049

Mt. Albert Markham
10,522

Mt. McClintock
11,457

TRANSANTARCTIC MOUNTAINS

ANTARCTICA

SØR RONDANE
MTS.

QUEEN FABIOLA
MTS.

VICTORIA LAND

CAMPBELL I. (N.Z.)

AUCKLAND IS.
(N.Z.)

MACQUARIE ISLAND
(Austl.)

South Magnetic Pole

GEORGE V COAST

WILKES LAND

ENDERBY
LAND

AMERICAN
HIGHLAND

LAMBERT GLACIER

AMERY
ICE SHELF

NAPIER MTS.

Cape
Ann

Cape
Darnley

PRINCE
EDWARD IS.
(S. Afr.)

Cape
Poinsett

ARCHIPEL
CROZET
(Fr.)

HEARD ISLAND
(Austl.)

ÎLES KERGUÉLEN
(Fr.)

Great Australian Bight

AUSTRALIA

Antarctic Circle

Antarctic Circle

Scale 1:45,000,000; one inch to 710 miles
Polar Sterographic Projection

0   200   400   600   800   1000 Miles
0   300   600   900   1200   1500 Kilometers

Index

Abbreviations of Geographical Names and Terms

Ak., U.S. ...... Alaska	Col. .... Colombia	H.K. ...... Hong Kong	Malay. ..... Malaysia	Nic. .... Nicaragua
Al., U.S. ...... Alabama	cont. .... continent	Hond. ...... Honduras	Md., U.S. .... Maryland	N.M., U.S. ... New Mexico
Ant. .... Antarctica	C.R. ...... Costa Rica		Me., U.S. .... Maine	N.S., Can. ... Nova Scotia
Ar., U.S. ...... Arkansas	ctry. .... country	i. .... island	Mex. .... Mexico	Nv., U.S. ..... Nevada
Arg. .... Argentina		Ia., U.S. ...... Iowa	Mi., U.S. .... Michigan	N.W.T., Can.
Asia .... Asia	D.C., U.S.	Id., U.S. ...... Idaho	Mn., U.S. .. Minnesota	Northwest Territories
Austl. .... Australia	District of Columbia	Il., U.S. ...... Illinois	Mo., U.S. .... Missouri	N.Y., U.S. ..... New York
Az., U.S. ...... Arizona	De., U.S. ..... Delaware	In., U.S. ...... Indiana	Monts. ...... Montserrat	N.Z. ...... New Zealand
	dep. .... dependency	Ire. .... Ireland	Mor. .... Morocco	
b. .... bay, gulf	Dom. Rep.	is. .... islands	Ms., U.S. .. Mississippi	Oh., U.S. ....Ohio
Bah. .... Bahrain	Dominican Republic		Mt., U.S. ..... Montana	Ok., U.S. .... Oklahoma
B.C., Can.		Jam. .... Jamaica	mtn. .... mountain	Ont., Can. ...... Ontario
British Columbia	El Sal. ... El Salvador		mts. .... mountains	Or., U.S. ..... Oregon
Bol. .... Bolivia	Eng., U.K. ..... England	Ks., U.S. ..... Kansas		
Braz. .... Brazil		Ky., U.S. .... Kentucky	N.A. .... North America	Pa., U.S. .. Pennsylvania
	Fl., U.S. ...... Florida		Nb., U.S. .....Nebraska	Pak. .... Pakistan
c. ....cape, point		l. .... lake	N.C., U.S. North Carolina	Pan. .... Panama
Ca., U.S. .... California	Ga., U.S. ......Georgia	La., U.S. ..... Louisiana	N.D., U.S. North Dakota	Para. .... Paraguay
Can. ....Canada	Guad. ...... Guadeloupe	Leb. .... Lebanon	Newf., Can. Newfoundland	pen. .... peninsula
Cay. Is. .. Cayman Islands			N.H., U.S. New Hampshire	Phil. .... Philippines
Co., U.S. ......Colorado	hist. reg. .. historic region	Ma., U.S. .. Massachusetts		

plat. .... plateau	Tn., U.S. ..... Tennessee
pol. div. ... political division	Trin.
P.R. ......Puerto Rico	Trinidad and Tobago
prov. .... province	Tx., U.S. ..... Texas
res. .... reservoir	U.K. .. United Kingdom
	Urug. ...... Uruguay
Sask., Can. Saskatchewan	U.S. ...... United States
S.C., U.S. South Carolina	Ut., U.S. ....Utah
Scot., U.K. .... Scotland	
S.D., U.S.	Va., U.S. ...... Virginia
South Dakota	Ven. ...... Venezuela
Sen. .... Senegal	vol. .... volcano
Sri L. ...... Sri Lanka	Vt., U.S. ..... Vermont
St. K./N.	
St. Kitts and Nevis	Wa., U.S. .... Washington
stm. ...... river, stream	Wi., U.S. .... Wisconsin
strt. ....strait	W.V., U.S. West Virginia
	Wy., U.S. .... Wyoming